4 MAN ON THE MOON

13 HOME

20 GONE, GONE, GONE

29 HOLD ON

37 TELL ME A STORY

47 GET UP GET DOWN

55 WHERE WE CAME FROM

63 DRIVE ME

72 WANTED IS LOVE

81 CAN'T GO WRONG

90 A FOOL'S DANCE

100 SO EASY

105 HAZEL

MAN ON THE MOON

Words and Music by
PHILLIP PHILLIPS

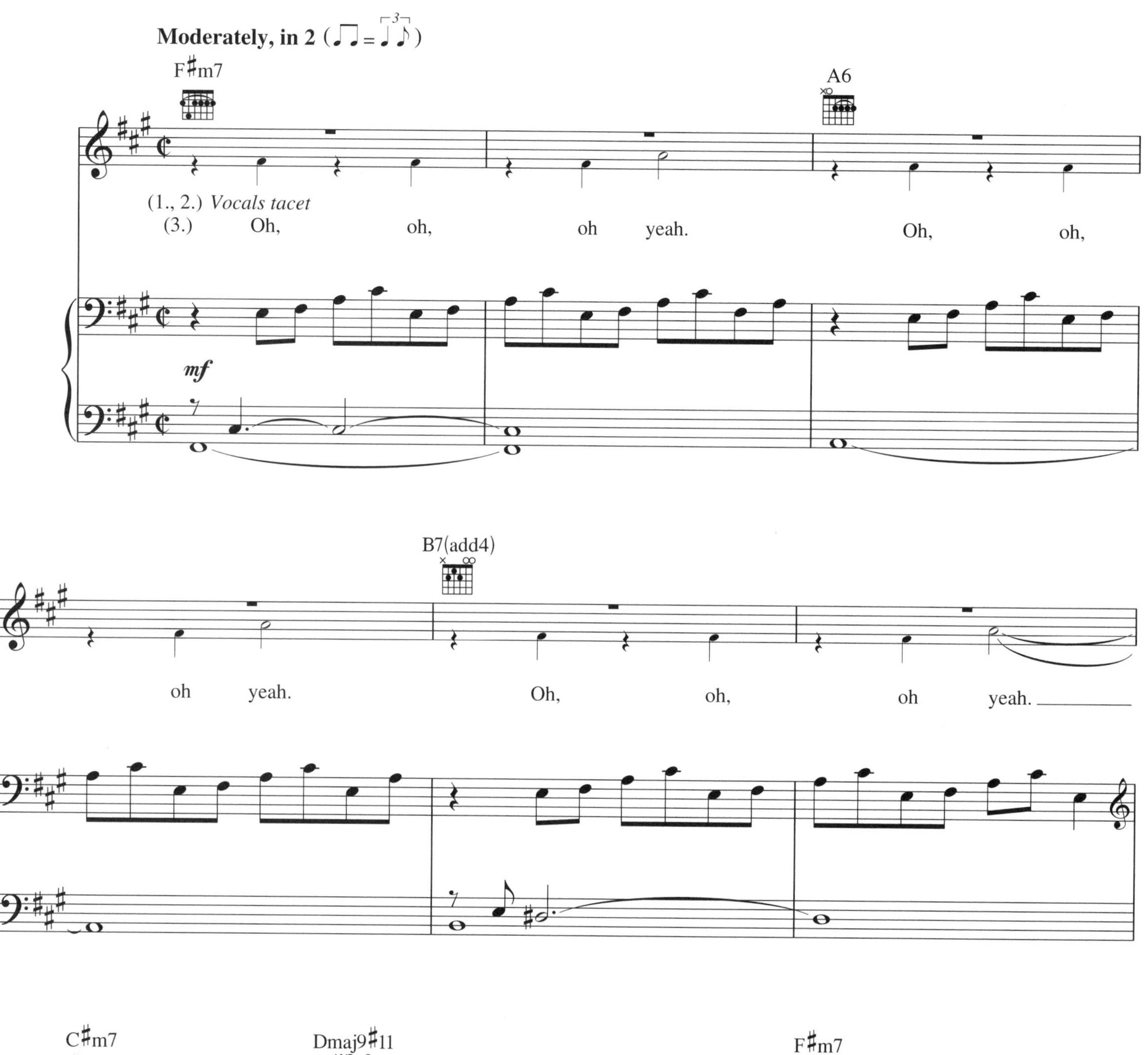

A6
from the side of the moon, looking at the stars, looking back to you
B7(add4)
C♯m7
Dmaj9♯11
just to see if you were still a-live, looking at the sun with the
F♯m7
fire in your eyes. It's hard to know where I stand; e-ven the
A6
B7(add4)
man in the moon couldn't tell me where to land. But I want-ed to

C#m7
4fr
Dmaj9#11
fly in this sea with no grav - i - ty to pull me down.
F#m7
Asus2
Esus
B
Hold on; it won't take long; you can find your - self if you de -
A
F#m7
Asus2
Esus
cide to fi - n'lly start. Don't look to me when you fall, 'cause the
B
A
F#m
steps get big - ger, so go a - head and walk them off. And you know

A
C♯m7
4fr
Dmaj7
how I feel,
so
F♯m
A(add2)
A/C♯
E
don't let your life start to

E(add4)
To Coda
slow - ly
waste a - way.

F♯m7
A6

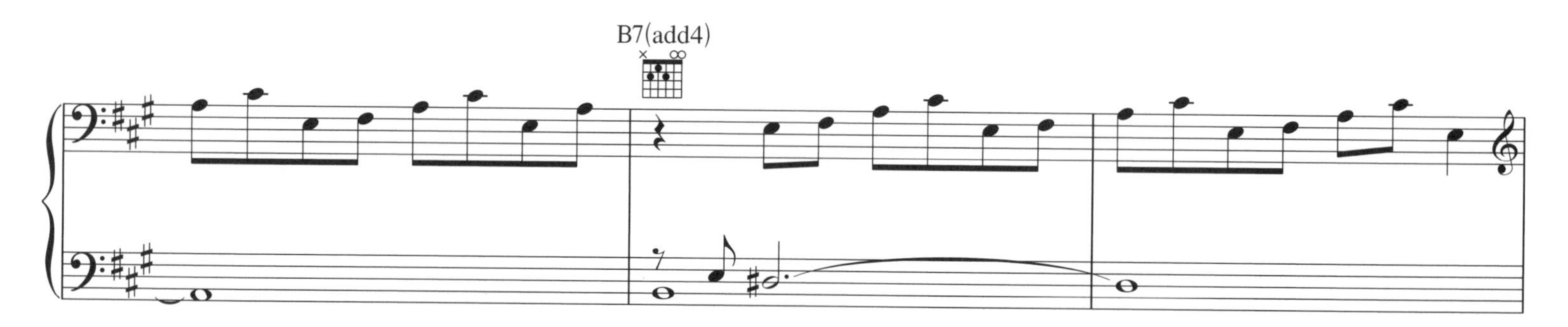
B7(add4)

C#m7
4fr
Dmaj9#11
F#m7
So, tell me this one thing. Now

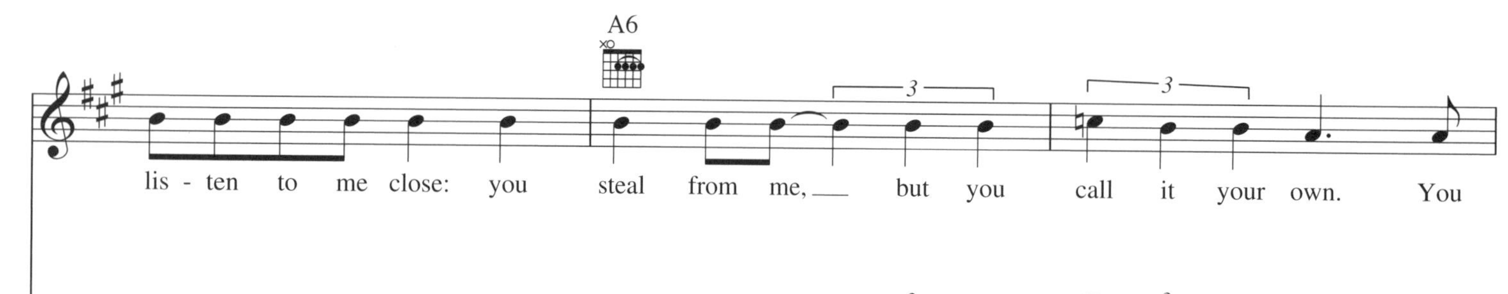
A6
3
lis - ten to me close: you steal from me, but you call it your own. You

3

B7(add4)
C#m7
4fr
Dmaj9#11
li - ar. You thief. Go make your stand on your own

F♯m7
two feet. So whoa, now, whoa, now, lis - ten what your friends say.
A6
B7(add4)
Go now, go now, go and do it that way. I'm the one you want
C♯m7
4fr
Dmaj9♯11
D.S. al Coda
to be - lieve, but in your heart you can see.
CODA
F♯m7
D♯m7♭5
6fr
Oh, let it
3

Dmaj13
5fr
fall,
let it
fall.

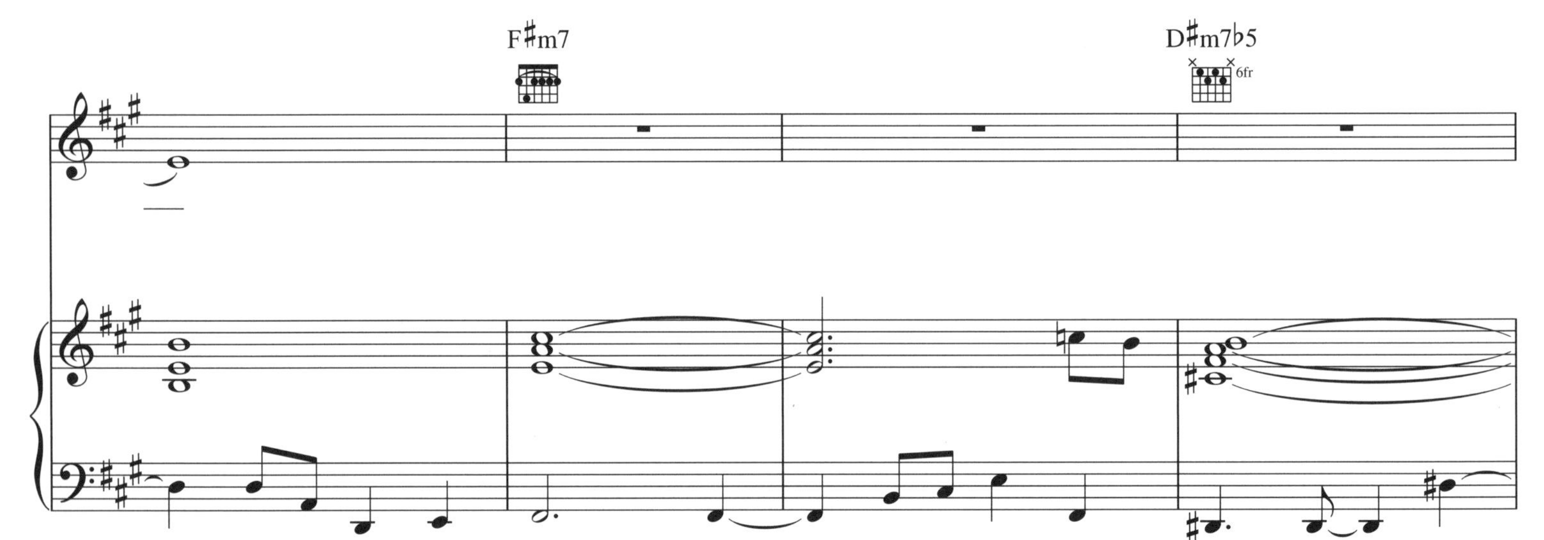
F♯m7
D♯m7♭5
6fr

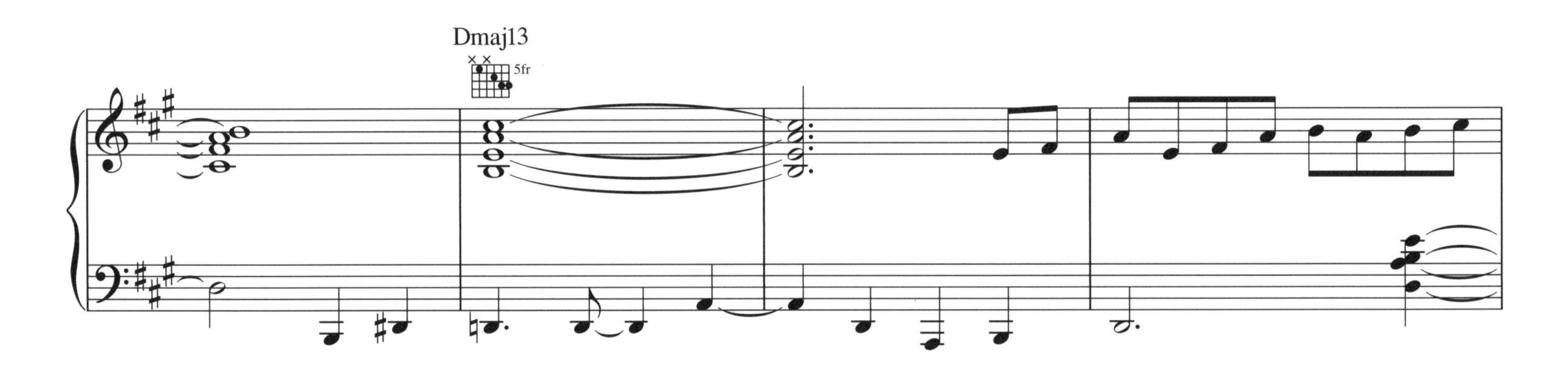
Dmaj13
5fr

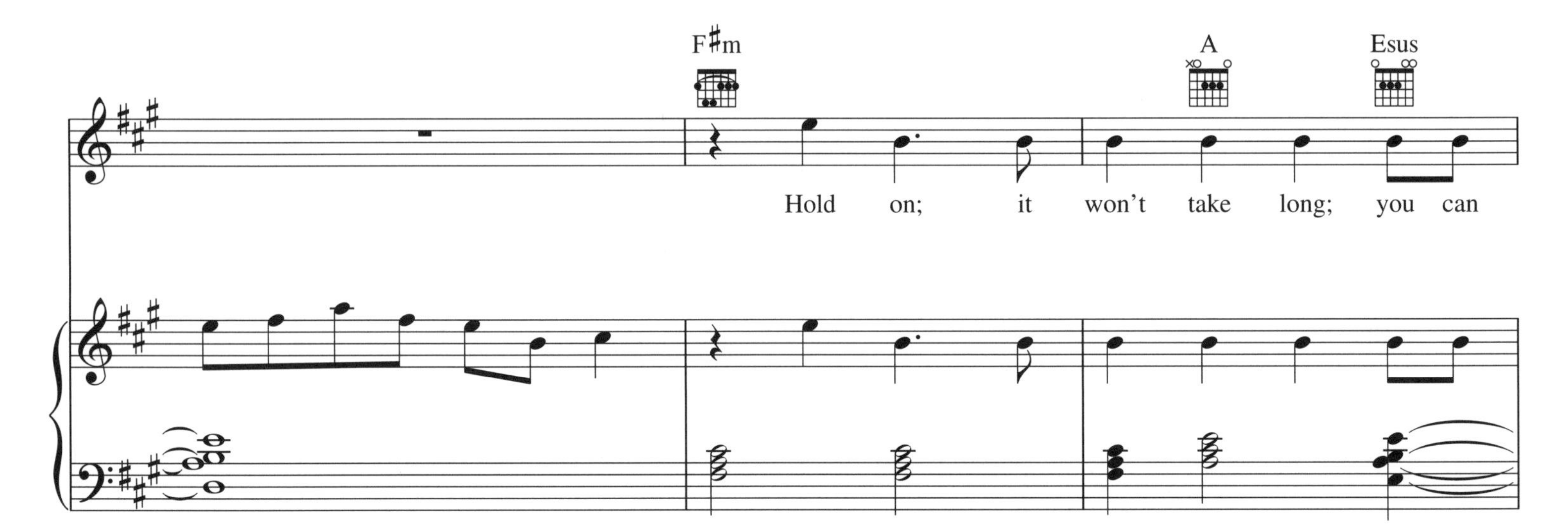
F♯m
A
Esus
Hold on; it won't take long; you can

B(add4)
F♯m
find your - self if you de - cide to fi - n'lly start. Don't look to me
A
Esus
B(add4)
when you fall, 'cause the steps get big - ger, so go a -
F♯m
A
C♯m7
4fr
head and walk them off. And you know how I
Dmaj7
F♯m
feel, so don't let your

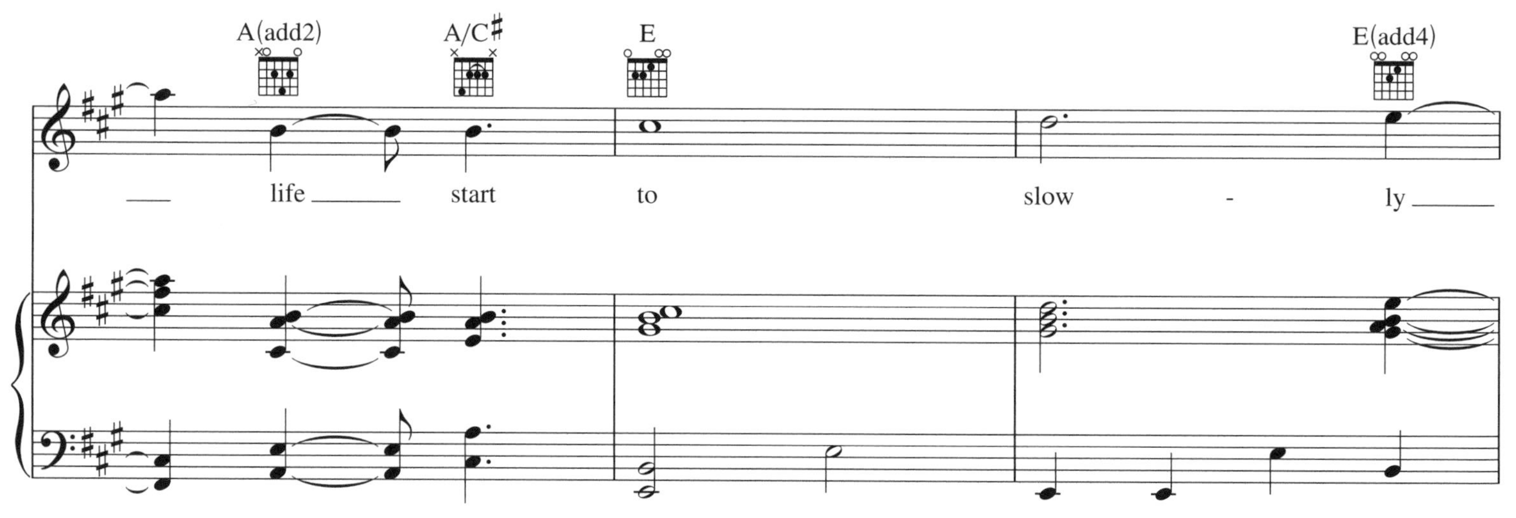
A(add2)
A/C#
E
E(add4)
life start to slow - ly

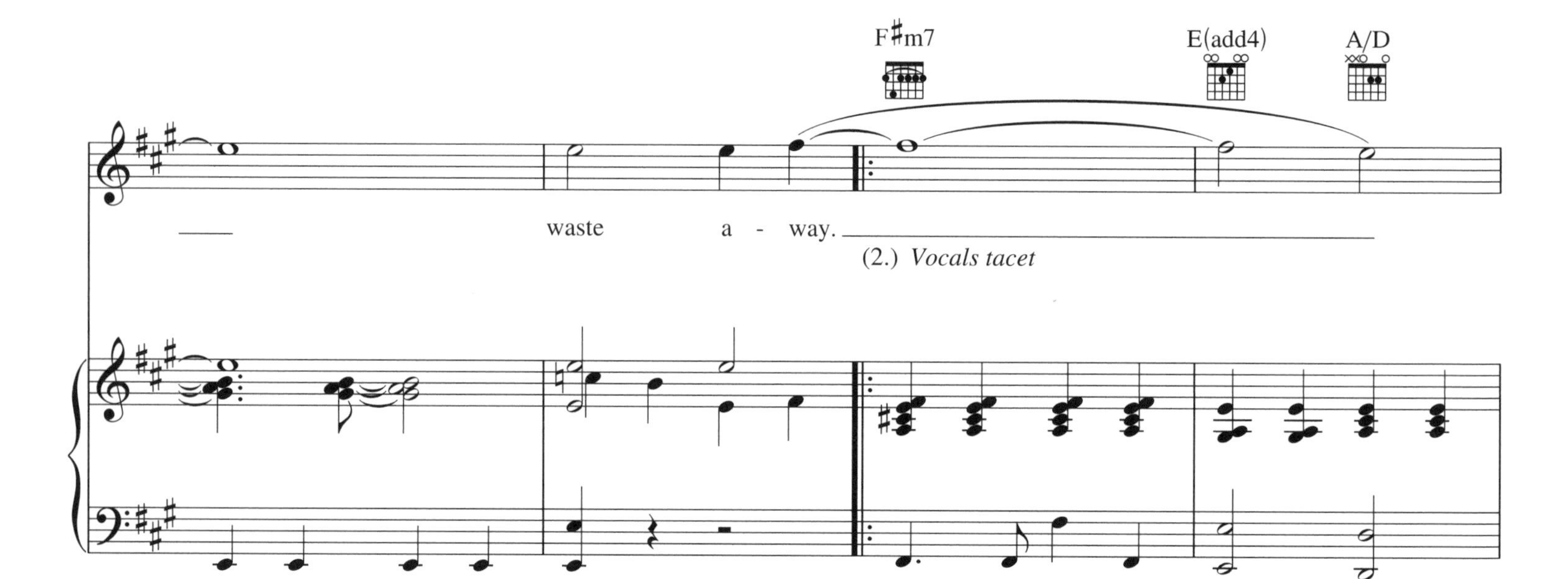
F#m7
E(add4)
A/D
waste a - way.
(2.) Vocals tacet

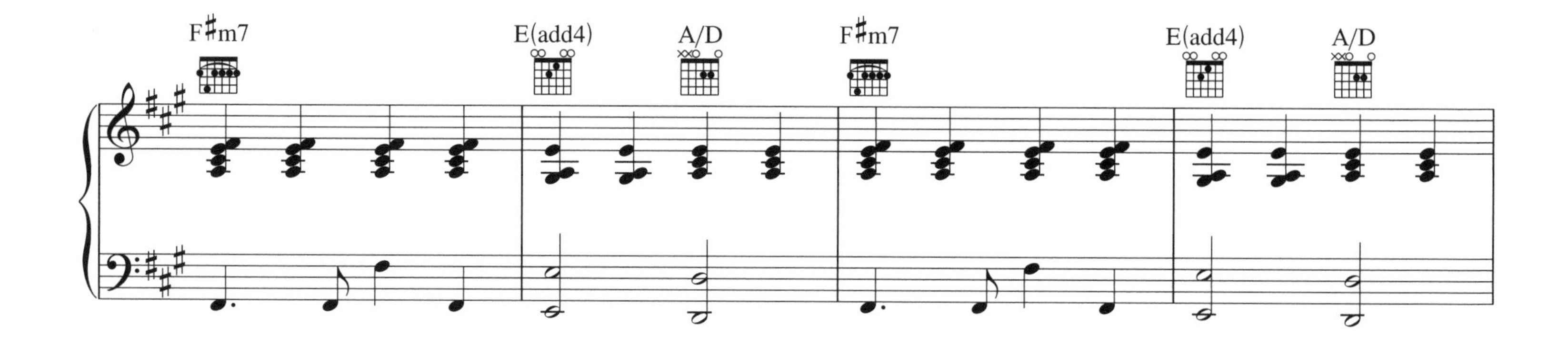
F#m7
E(add4)
A/D
F#m7
E(add4)
A/D

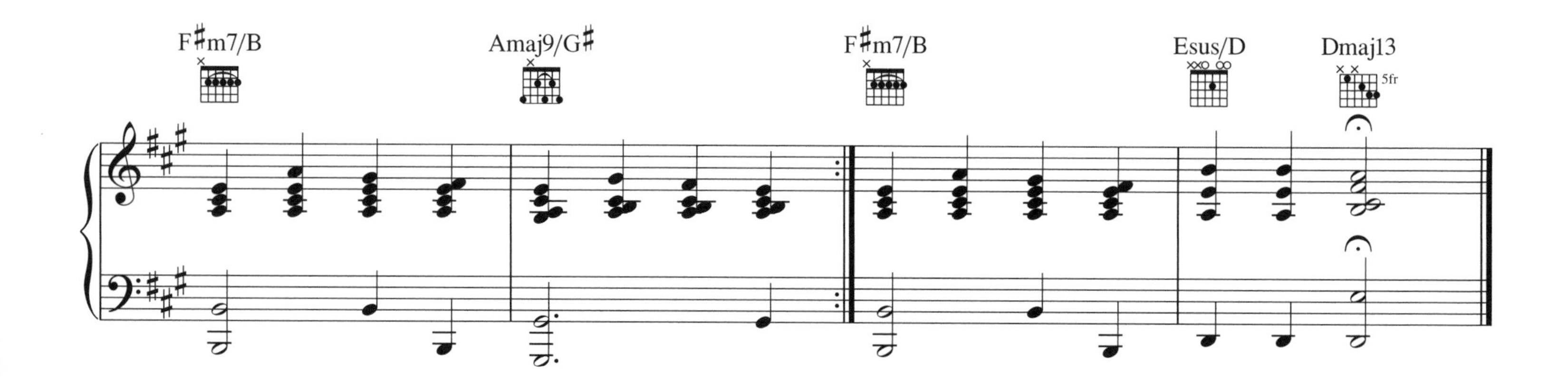
F#m7/B
Amaj9/G#
F#m7/B
Esus/D
Dmaj13
5fr

HOME

Words and Music by GREG HOLDEN
and DREW PEARSON

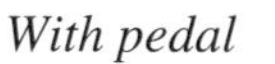

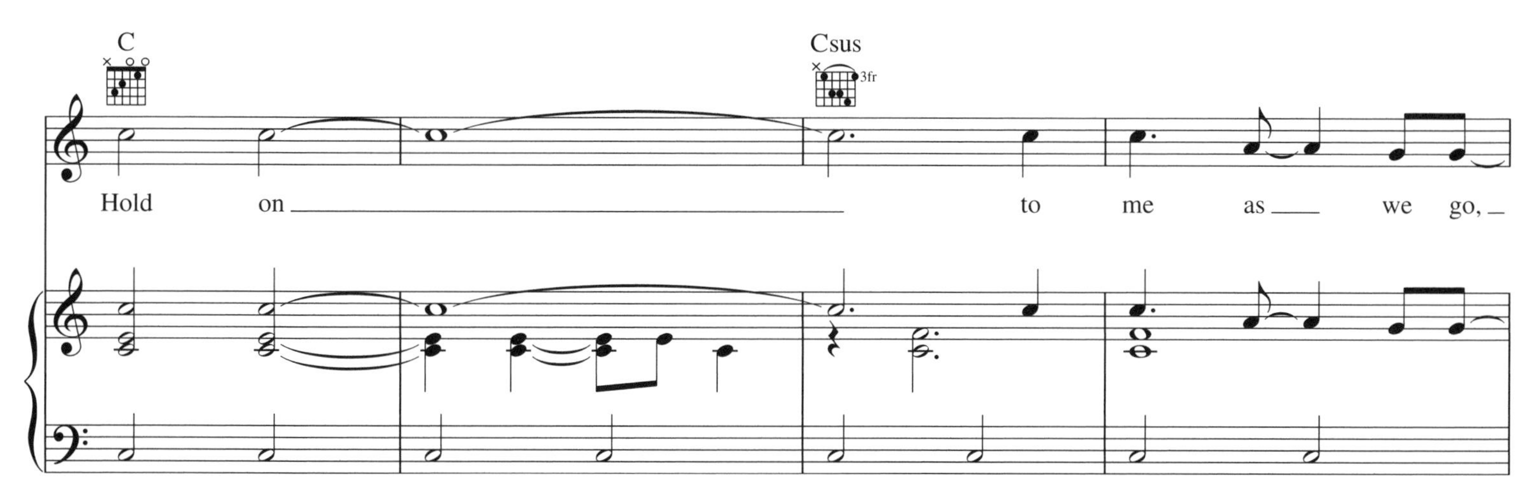

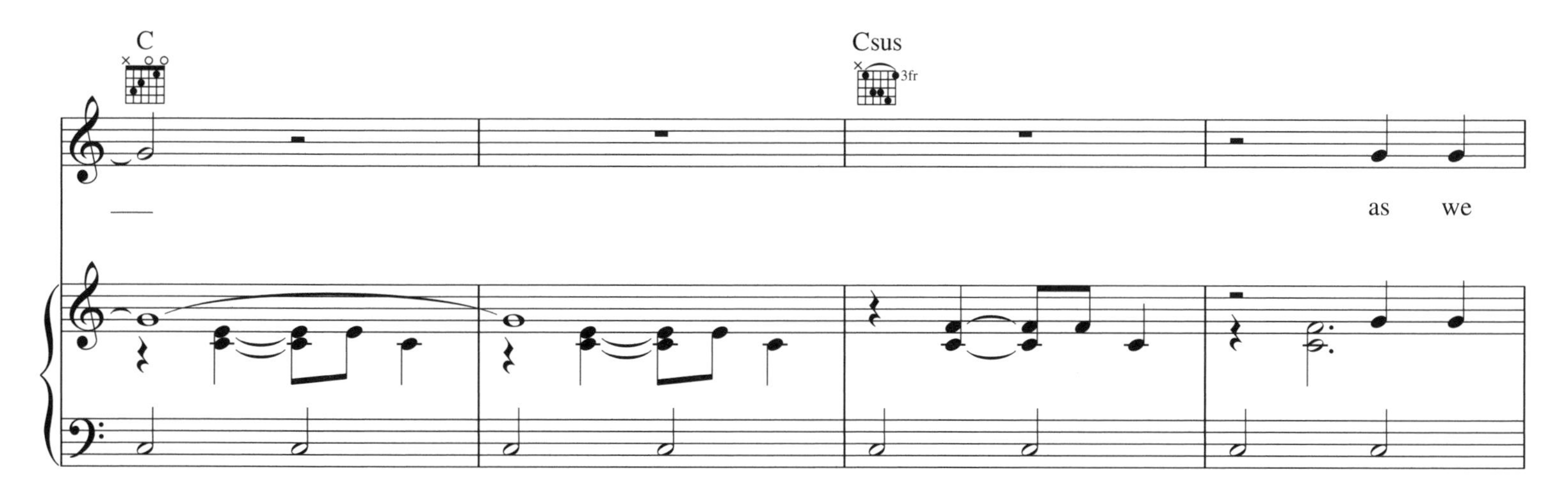

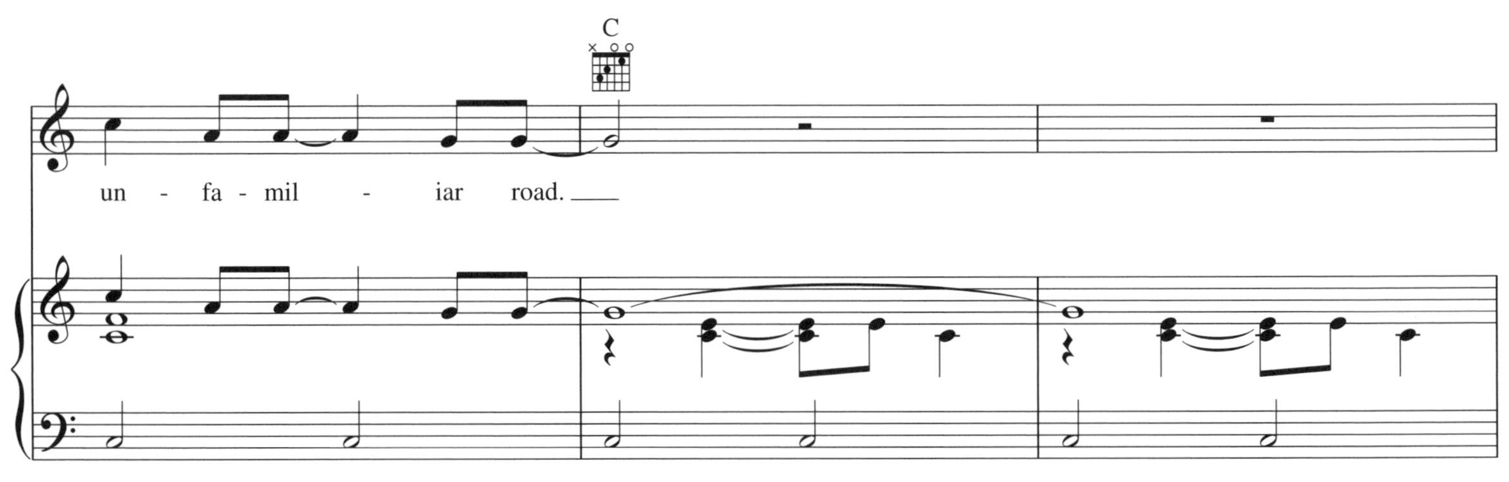
C
un - fa - mil - iar road.

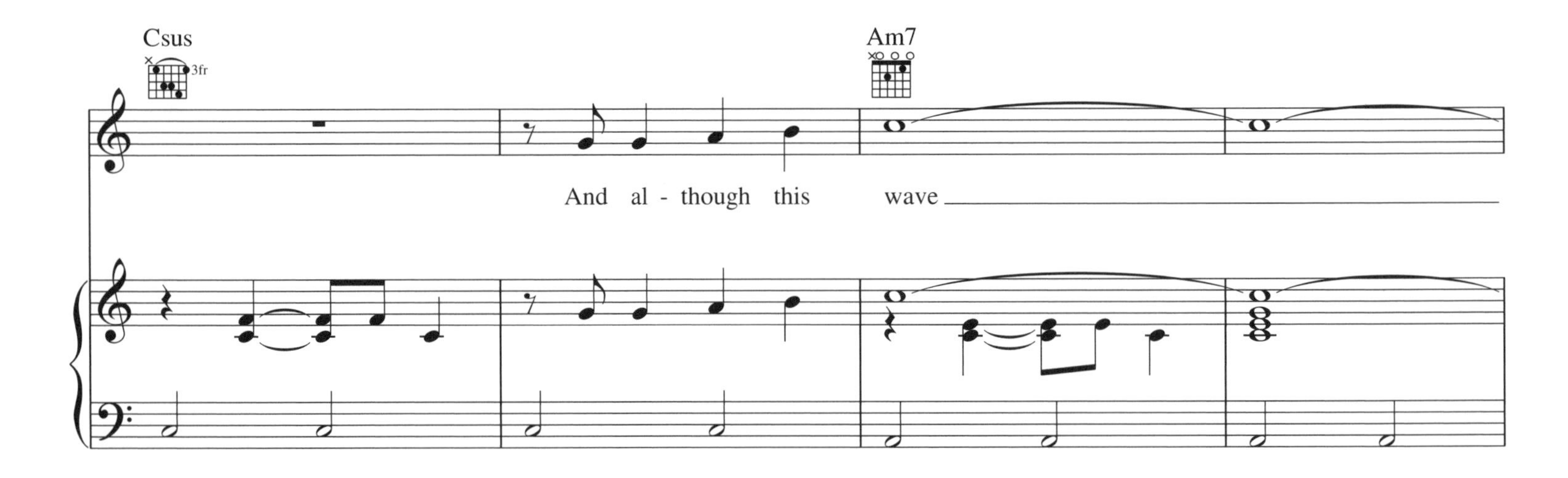
Csus
3fr
Am7
And al - though this wave

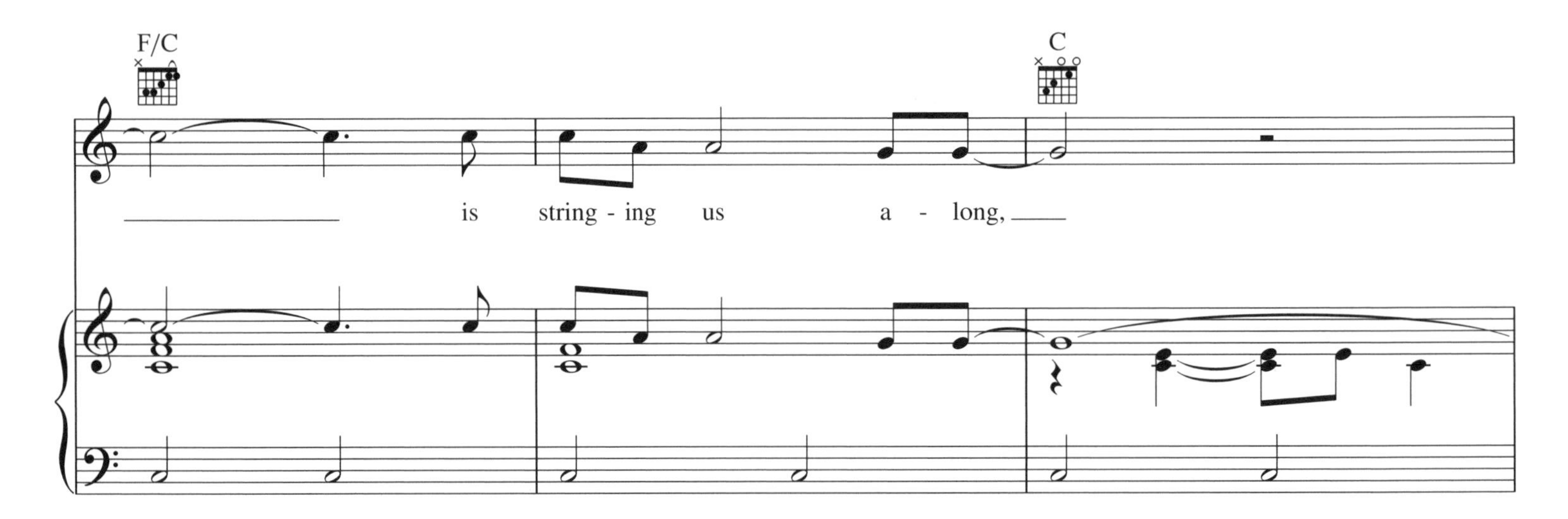
F/C
C
is string - ing us a - long,

Csus
3fr
C
C/B
just know you're

F/A
C/G
Am
not a - lone,
'cause I'm gon - na

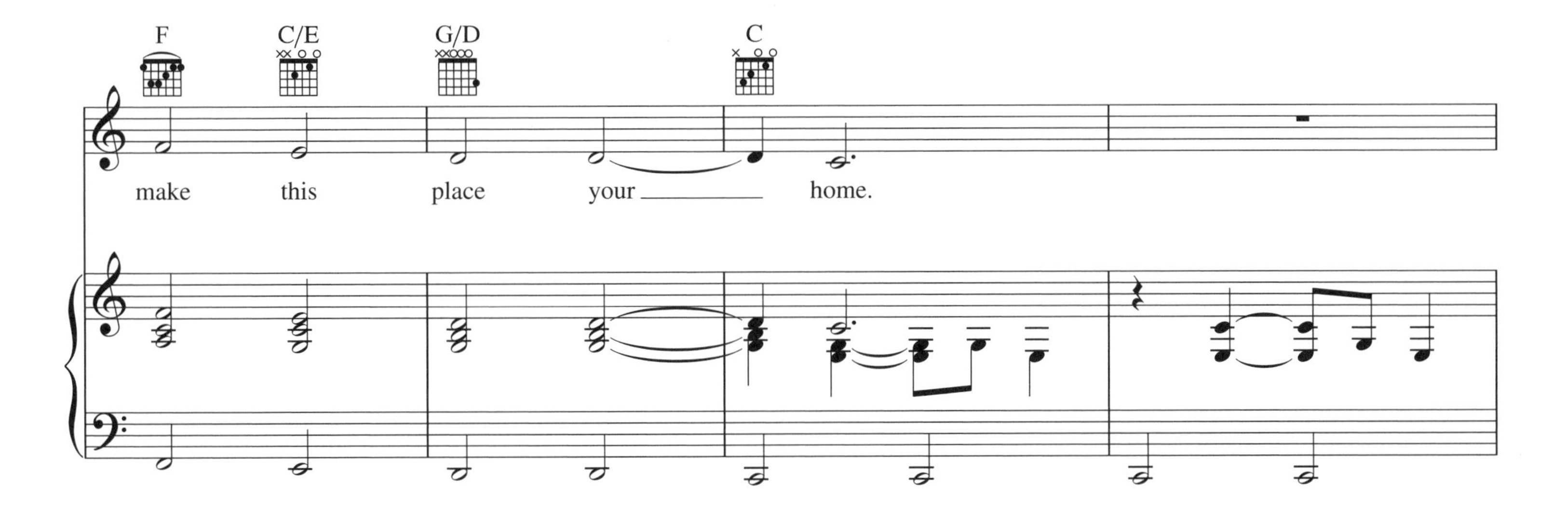
F
C/E
G/D
C
make this place your home.

C
Set - tle down,

Csus
3fr
C
it - 'll all be clear.

Csus
3fr
C
Don't pay no

Csus
3fr
C
mind to the de - mons; they fill you with fear.

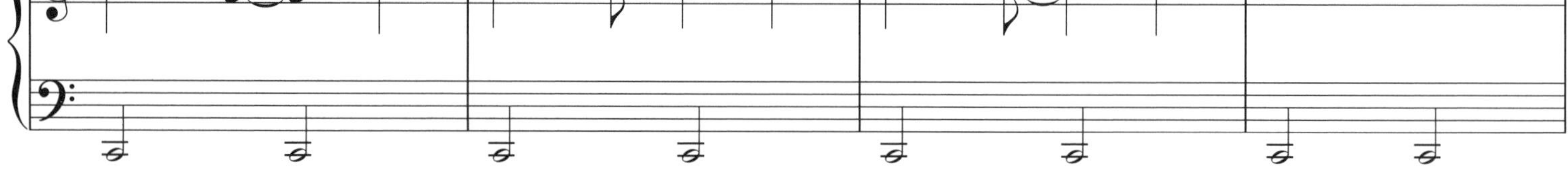

Csus
3fr
Am7
Trou - ble, it

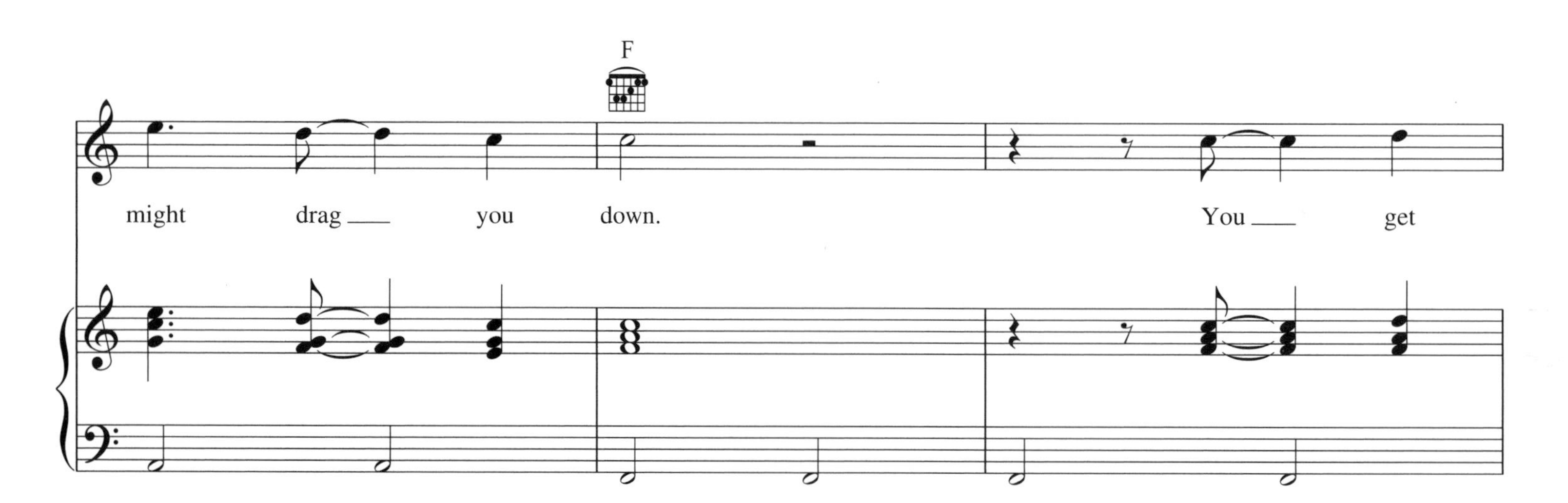
F
might drag you down. You get

C
G
lost, you can al - ways be found.
Just

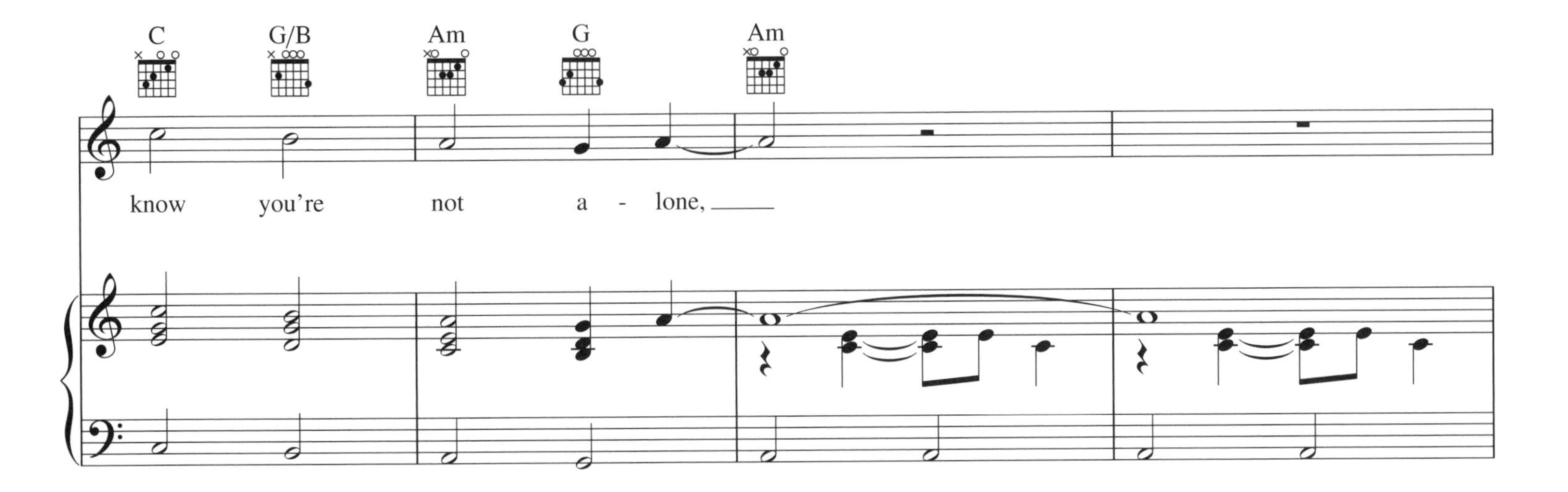
C
G/B
Am
G
Am
know you're not a - lone,

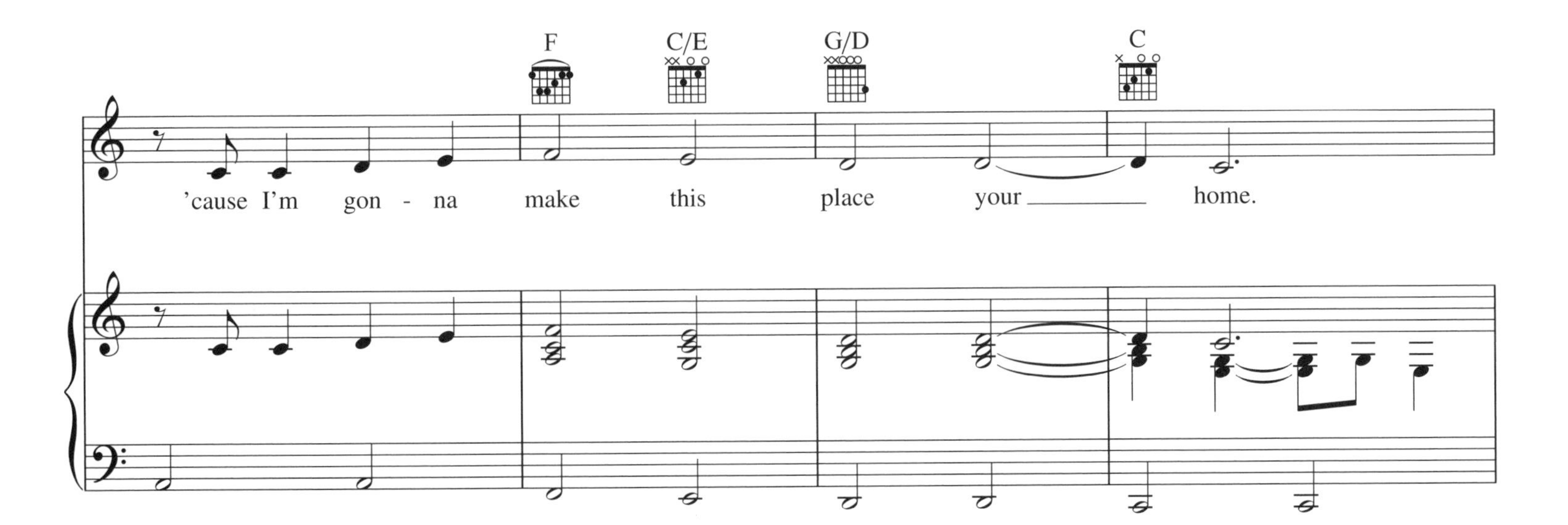
F
C/E
G/D
C
'cause I'm gon - na make this place your home.

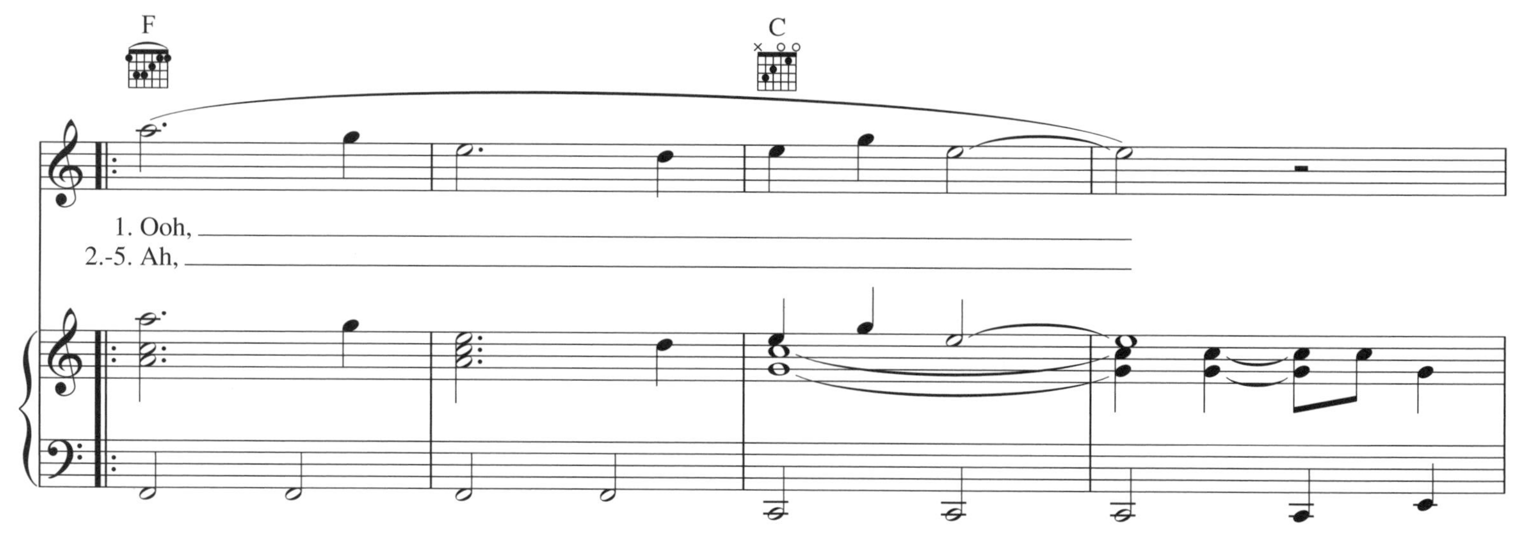
F
C
1. Ooh,
2.-5. Ah,

Am
G
ooh.
ah.

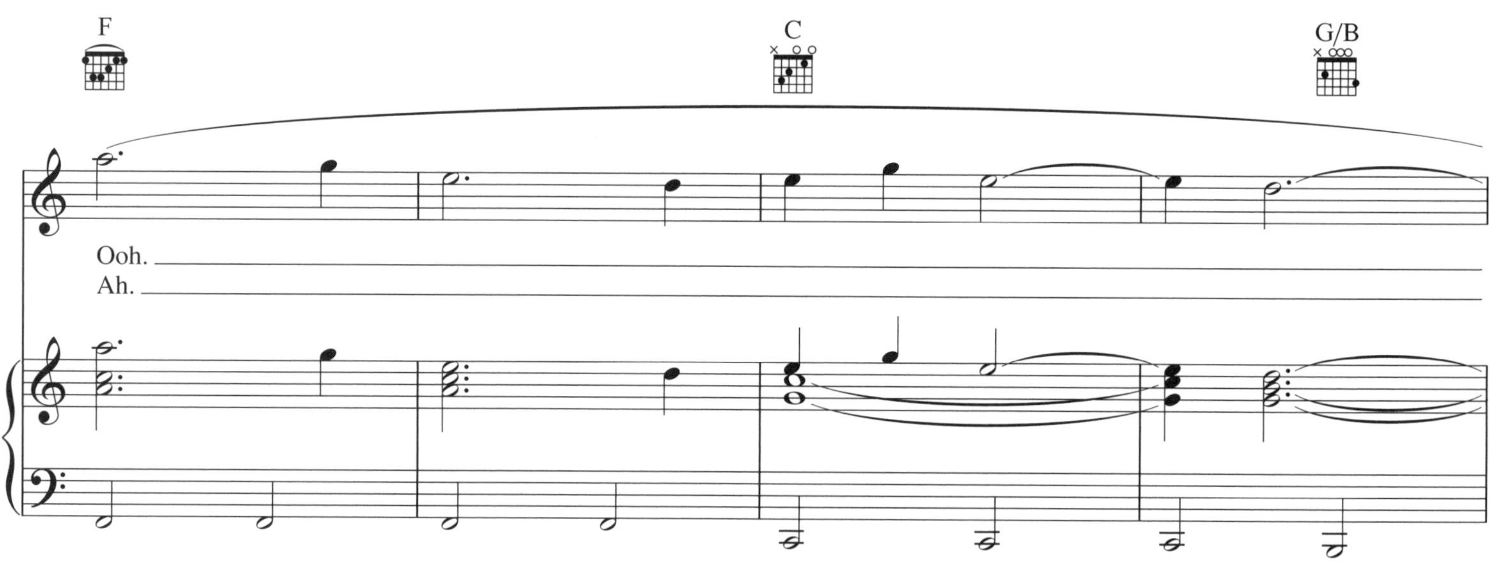
F
C
G/B
Ooh.
Ah.

G
Gsus
3fr
1, 2, 4
G

3
G
D.S.
5
G
F
Ah,

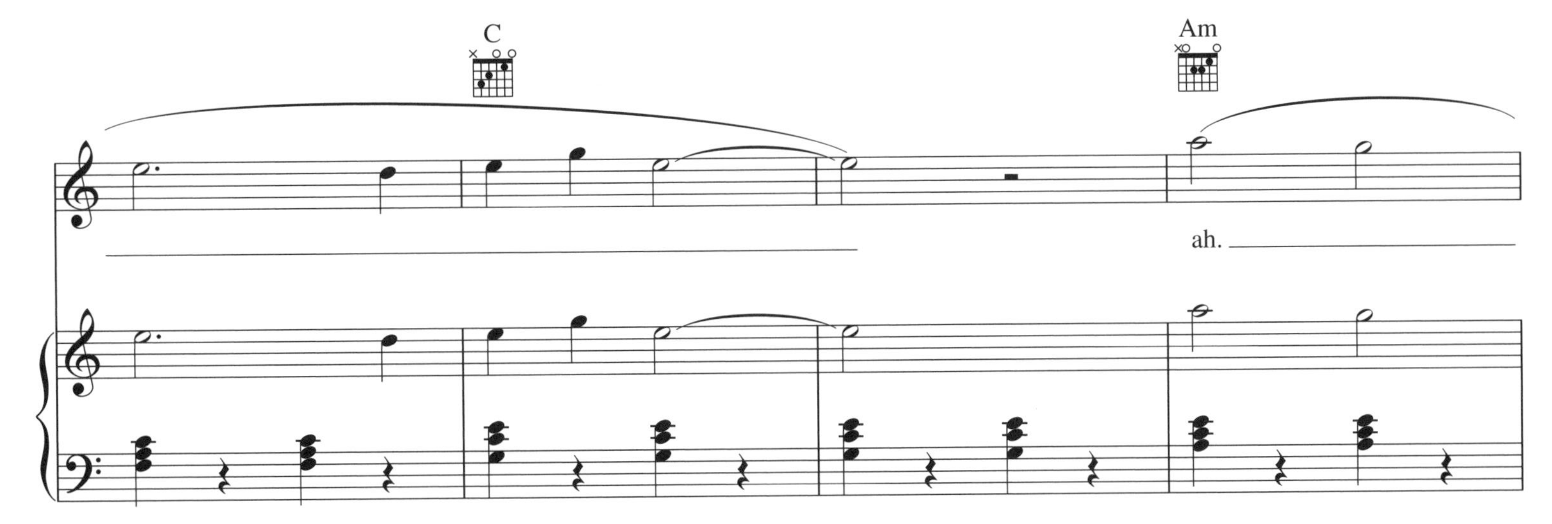
C
Am
ah.

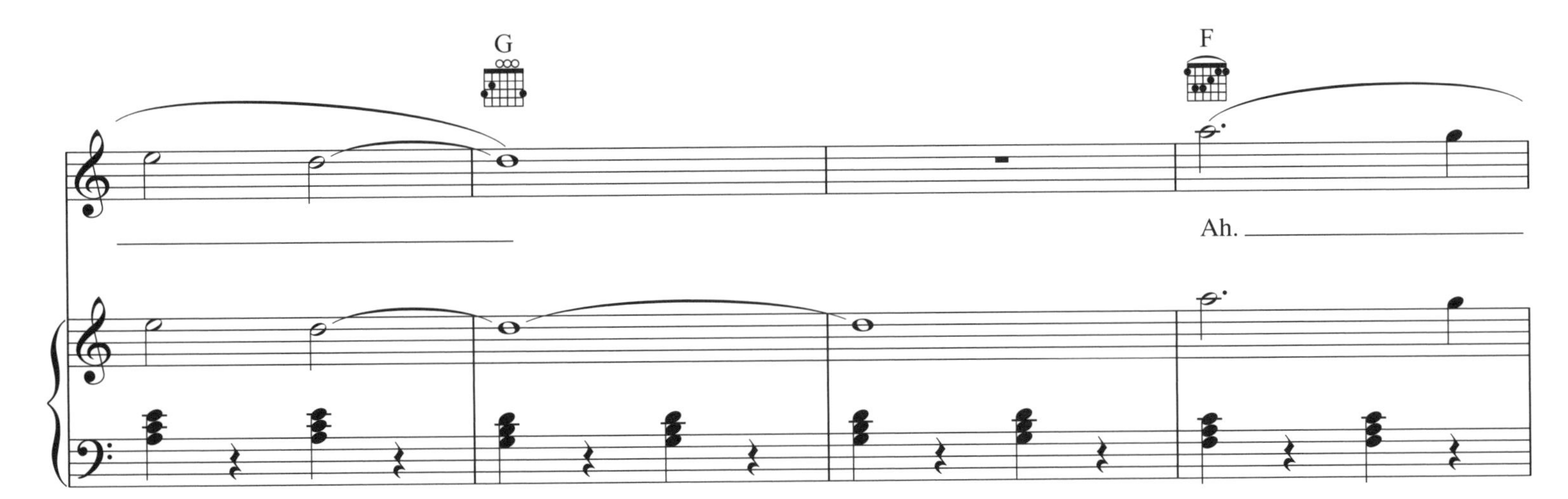
G
F
Ah.

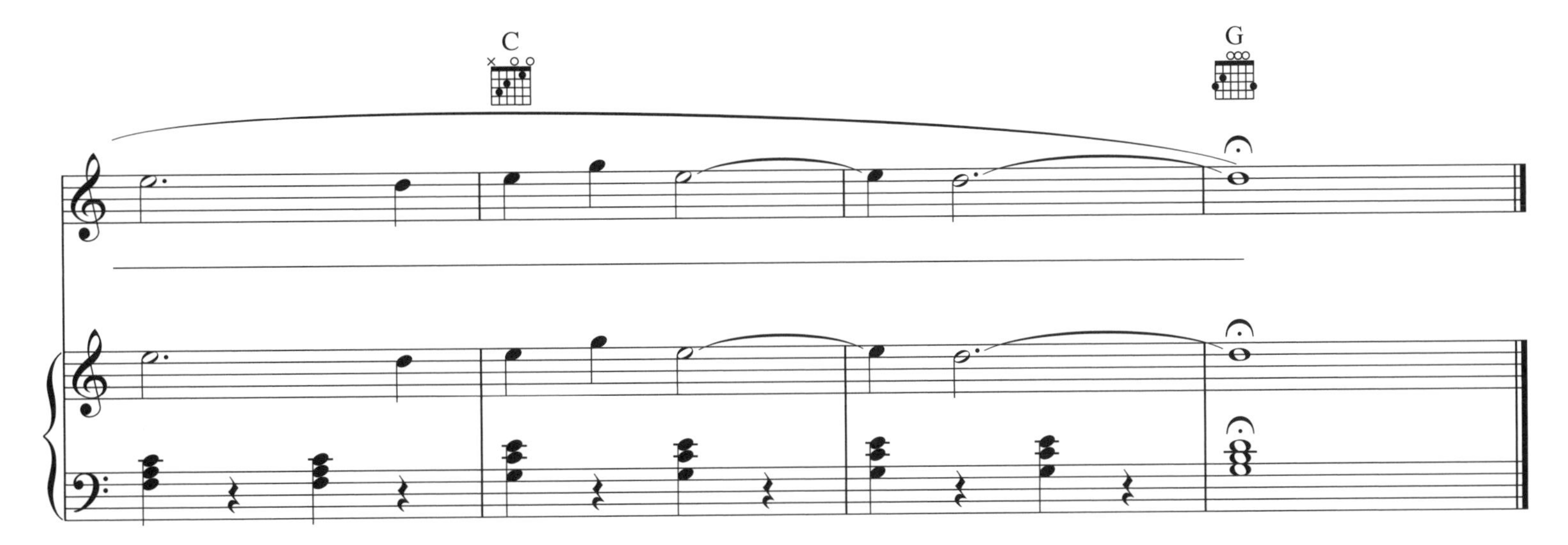
C
G

GONE, GONE, GONE

Words and Music by GREGG WATTENBERG,
DEREK FUHRMANN and TODD CLARK

*Recorded a half step higher.

Dm7
shut down the cit - y lights, I'll lie, cheat, I'll beg and bribe to
B♭sus2
make you well, to make you well. When
F5
en - e - mies are at your door, I'll car - ry you a - way from war if
fall like a sta - tue, I'm gon' be there to catch you, put you
Csus
3fr
you need help, if you need help. Your
on your feet, you on your feet. and if

Dm7
hope dan - gling by a string, I'll share in your suf - fer - ing to
your world is emp - ty, not a thing will pre - vent me. Tell me
B♭(add2)
3fr
make you well, to make you well. Give me
what you need. What do you need? I sur -
B♭
F
C
B♭
F
rea - sons to be - lieve that you would do the same for
ren - der hon - est - ly; you've al - ways done the same for
C
B♭
F
me. And } I will do it (for you, for
me. So }

Dm7
C
B♭
F
you.)
Ba - by, I'm not mov - ing on, I'll love you long
Dm7
C
B♭
F
af - ter you're gone. (For you, for
Dm7
C
B♭
F
you.)
You will nev - er sleep a - lone; I'll love you long
Dm7
C
1
af - ter you go, and long af - ter you're gone, gone,

F5
gone.
When you
2
long af - ter you're gone, gone, gone.
Dm7
You're my back - bone,
F
you're my cor - ner - stone,
B♭sus2
you're my crutch when my
B♭(add2)
3fr
legs stop mov - ing.
Dm7
You're my head start,

F
Bb sus2
you're my rug - ged heart, you're the pulse that I've
Bb(add2)
3fr
Bb sus2
F
al - ways need - ed. Like a drum, ba - by,
Dm7
Csus
3fr
Bb sus2
F
don't stop beat - in'. Like a drum, ba - by,
Dm7
Csus
3fr
Bb sus2
F
don't stop beat - in'. Like a drum, ba - by,

Dm7
Csus
B♭sus2
F
don't stop beat - in'. Like a drum, my heart
Dm7
Csus
B♭
F
nev - er stops beat - in' (for you, for
Dm7
C
B♭
F
you.) Ba - by, I'm not mov - ing on, I'll love you long
Dm7
C
B♭
F
af - ter you're gone. (For you, for

Dm7
C
1
B♭
F
you.)
You will
nev - er
sleep a - lone;
I'll love you long

Dm7
C
2
B♭
F
af - ter you go.
(For
nev - er
sleep a - lone;
I'll love you long,

Dm7
C
N.C.
long
af - ter you go.
Like a drum,
ba - by,

don't stop beat - in'.
Like a drum,
ba - by,

don't stop beat - in'. Like a drum, ba - by, don't stop beat - in'.
Like a drum, my heart nev - er stops beat - in' for
you. And long af - ter you're gone, gone,
gone, I'll love you long af - ter you're gone, gone, gone.
F5
F/A
G7sus
rit.

HOLD ON

Words and Music by
PHILLIP PHILLIPS

Moderately, in 2

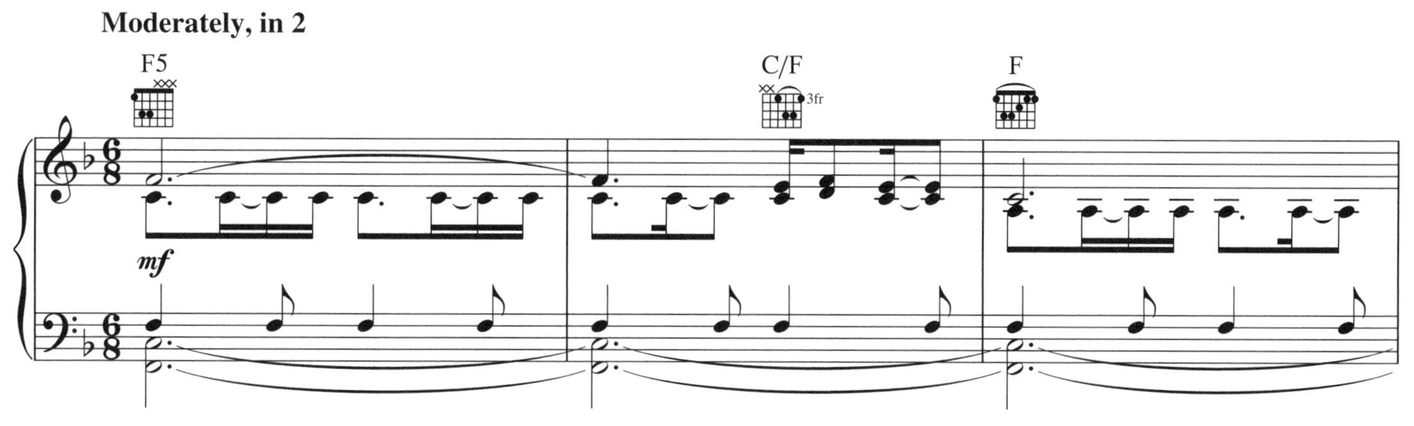

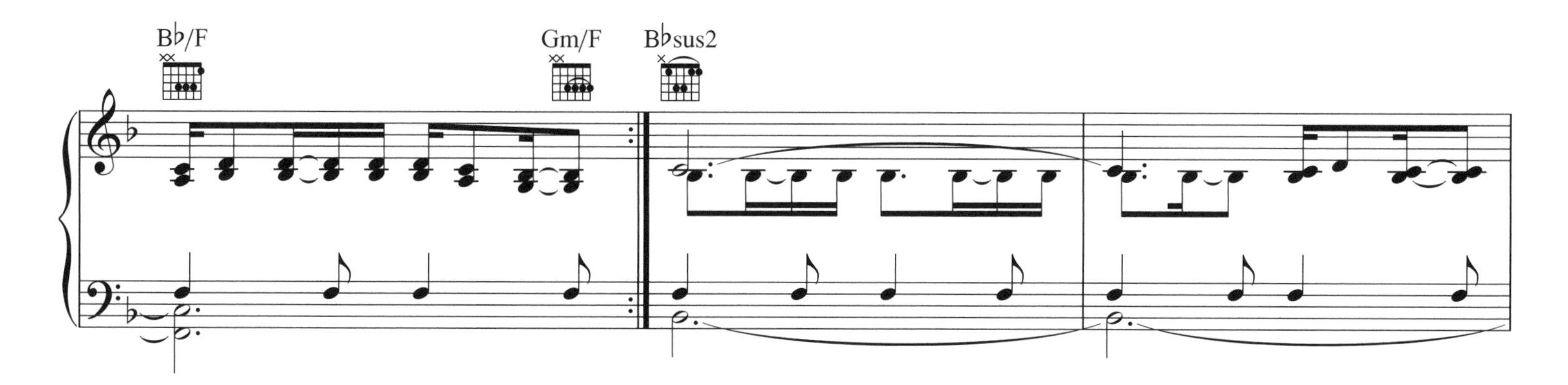

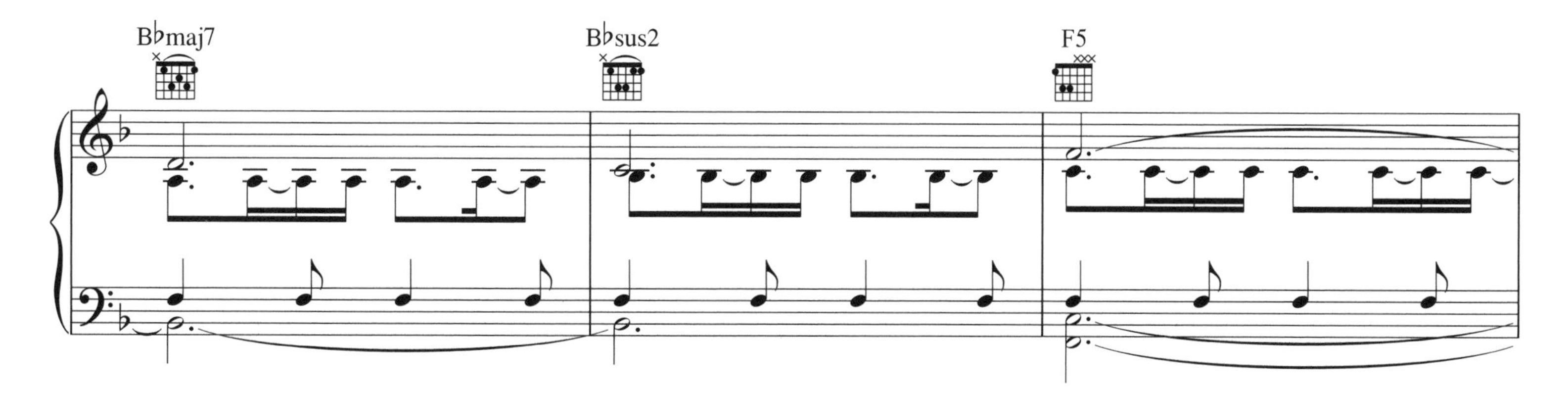

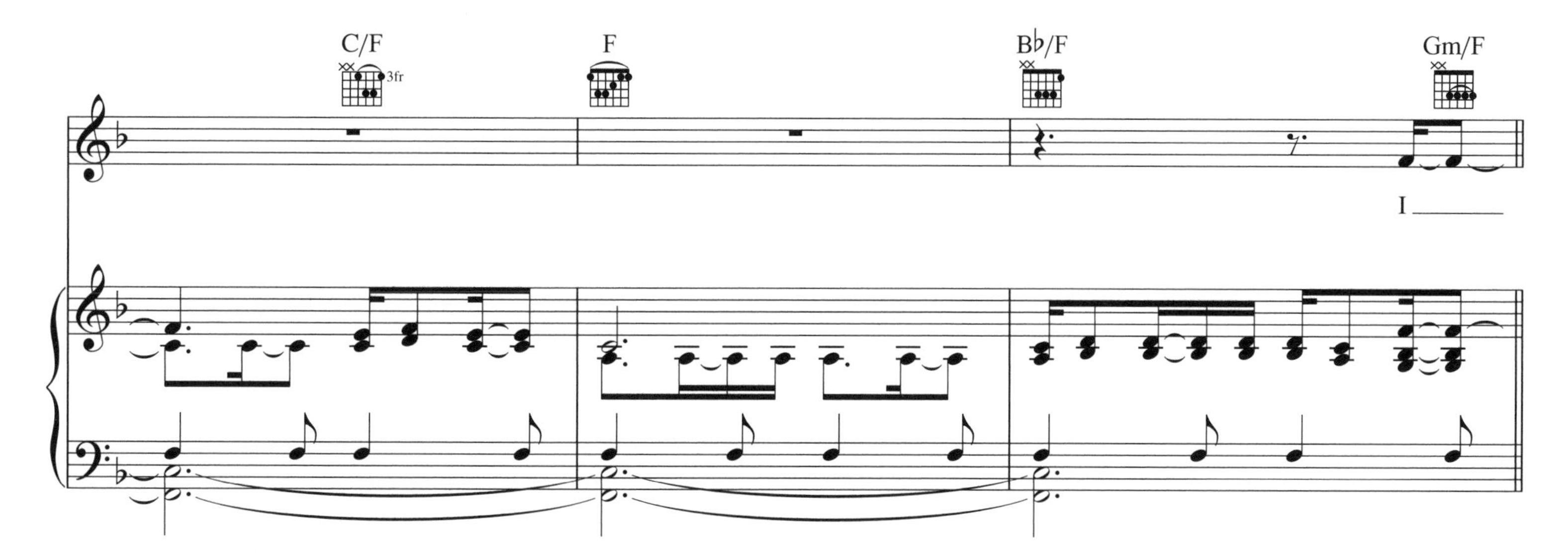

F5
C/F
3fr
F
fall in - to a sa - cred rage to es - cape
say, "You'll find your - self one of these days,"
B♭/F
Gm/F
F5
C/F
3fr
the hells of the world, made of pup - pets, and
as if they know I'm lost and can nev - er be
F
B♭/F
Gm/F
B♭sus2
fake. Death won't be
saved. A gam - ble is
B♭(add2)
3fr
B♭sus2
too far now; the seeds in my heart start to
what I'll take, trad - ing ash - es for gold, hop - ing life will give

F
C/F
3fr
F
a - wake.
its sake.
B♭/F
Gm/F
B♭sus2
So all I can do is be
Life is too short to stop
B♭
B♭sus2
F
the man that the Lord brought me to to - day.
and stare at the blank page that tells your way.
C/F
3fr
F
B♭/F
F
Na,

Dm11
3fr
C5
3fr
ooh,
ooh,
ooh,
F/A
ooh,
ooh.
Dm9
3fr
G7sus
Hold
on
B♭sus2
Fmaj9/A
Dm9
3fr
C(add4)
to
your
life
by

B♭(add2)
3fr
C13sus
8fr
Fmaj7/A
Gm9
3fr
love, and then you'll
C7/A
Dm9
find what's in
C(add4)
5fr
and out of line.
To Coda
B♭maj9
B♭6/9
F5
C/F
Just hold on.

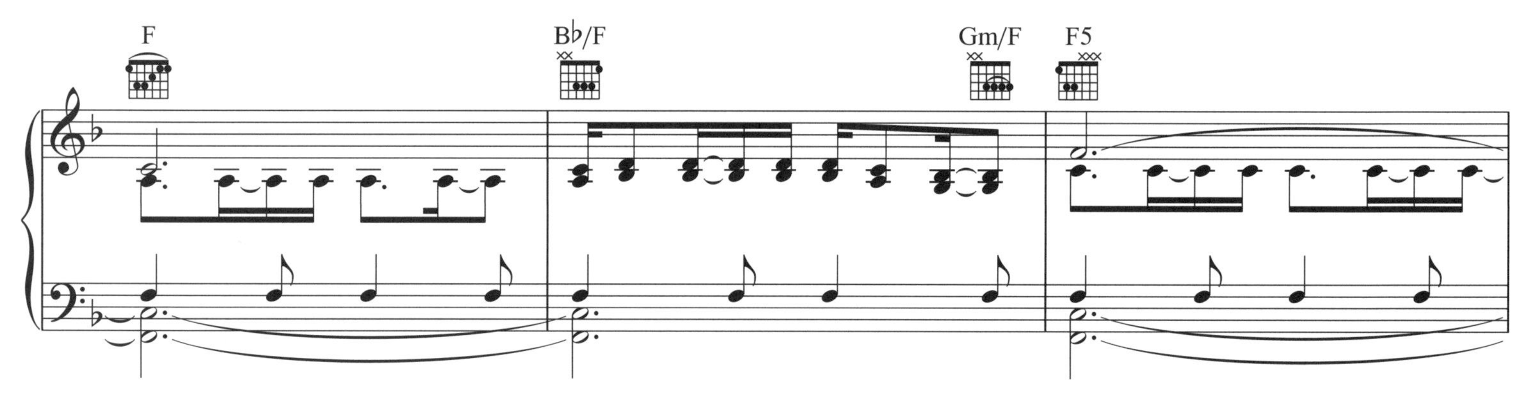
F
B♭/F
Gm/F
F5

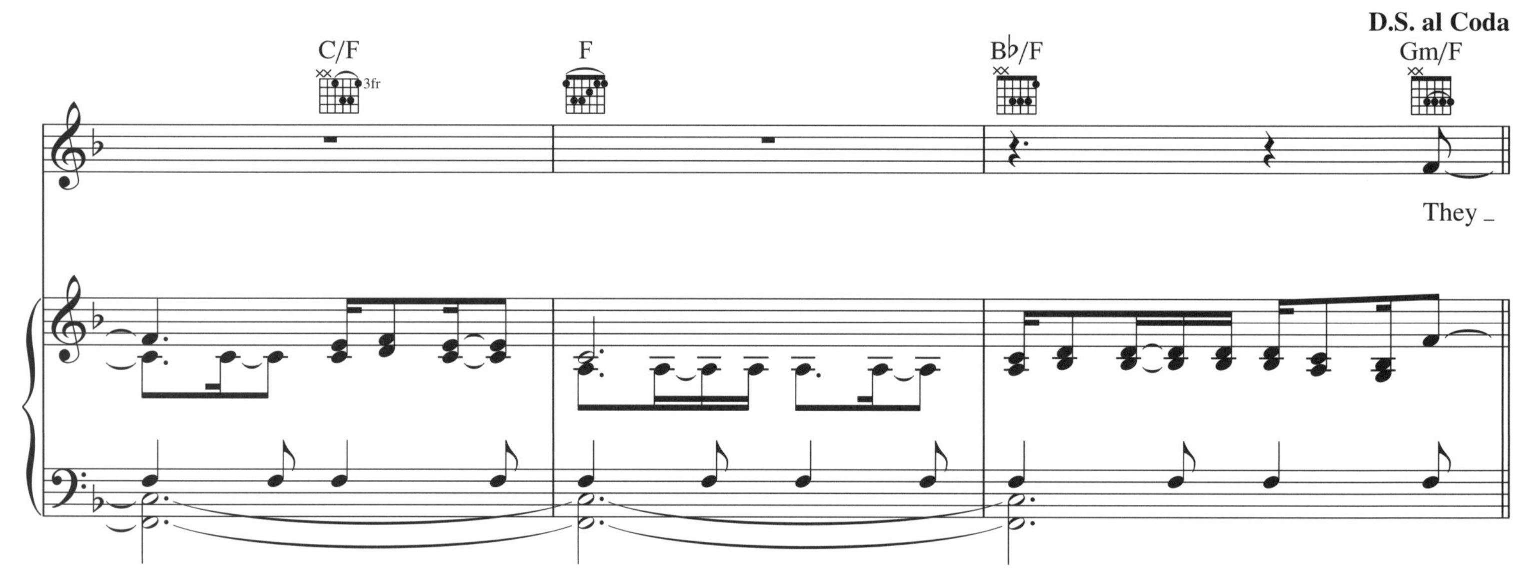
D.S. al Coda
C/F
F
B♭/F
Gm/F
3fr
They

CODA
B♭maj9
B♭6/9
F5
5fr
Just hold on.

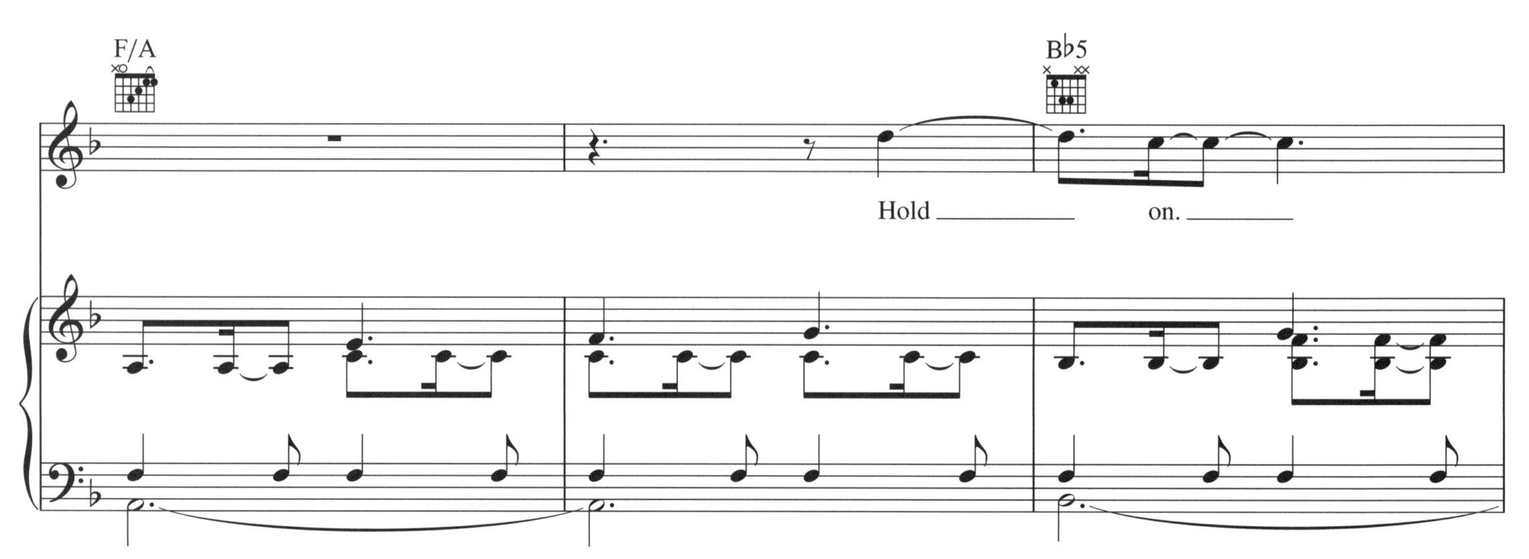
F/A
B♭5
Hold on.

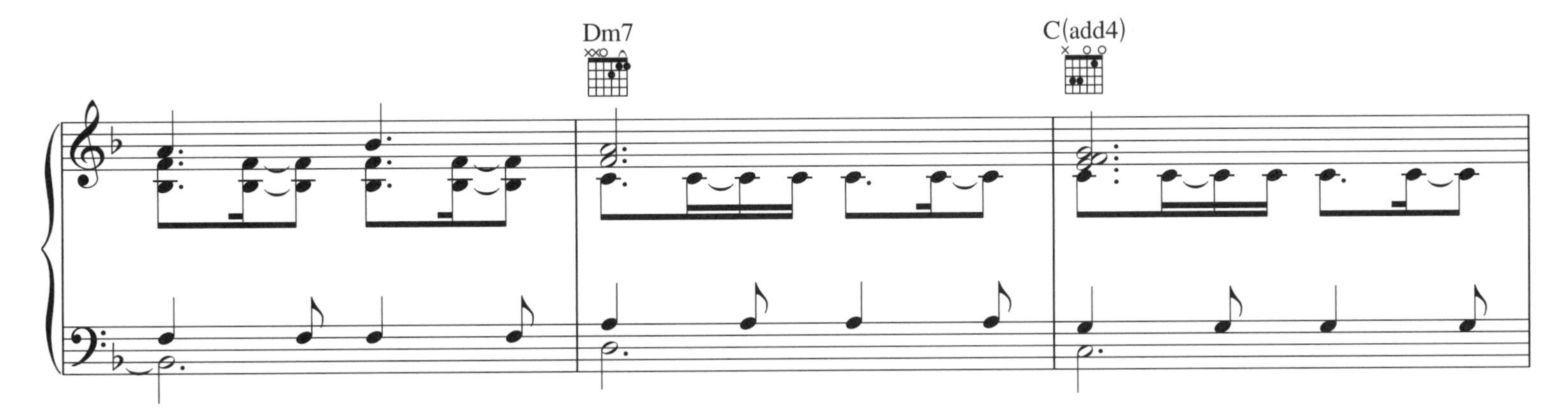
Dm7
C(add4)

F

F/A
B♭5

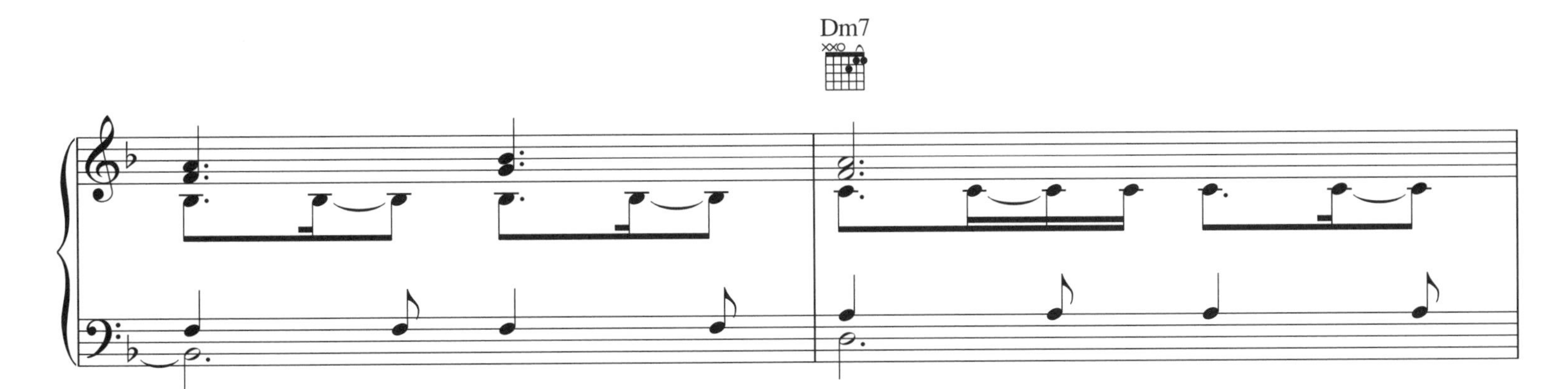
Dm7

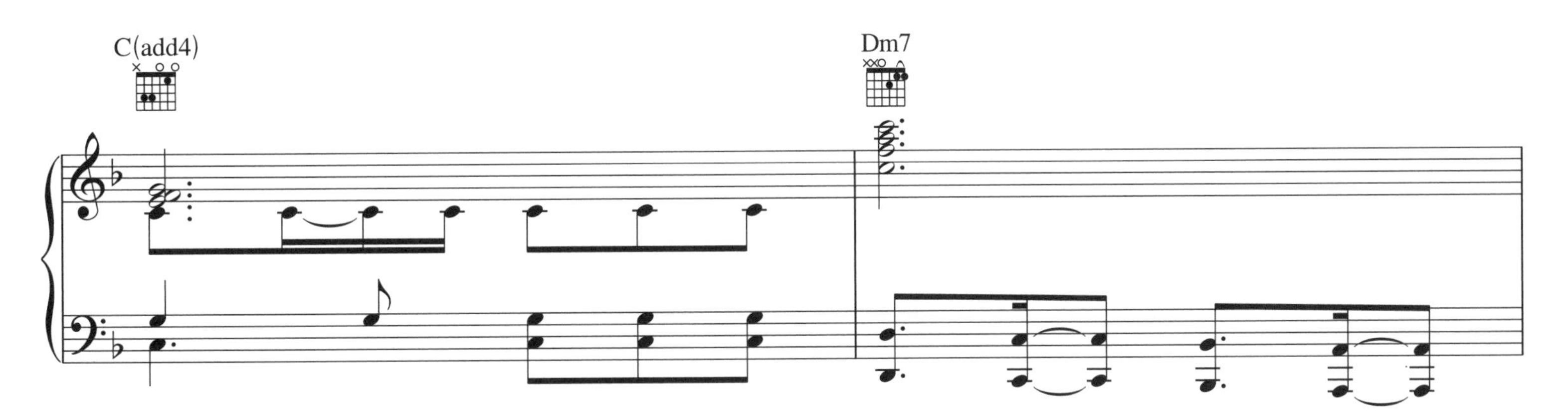
C(add4)
Dm7

Gm11
C(add4)
Y - yeah,

C(add4)
C(add4)
ah,
oh,

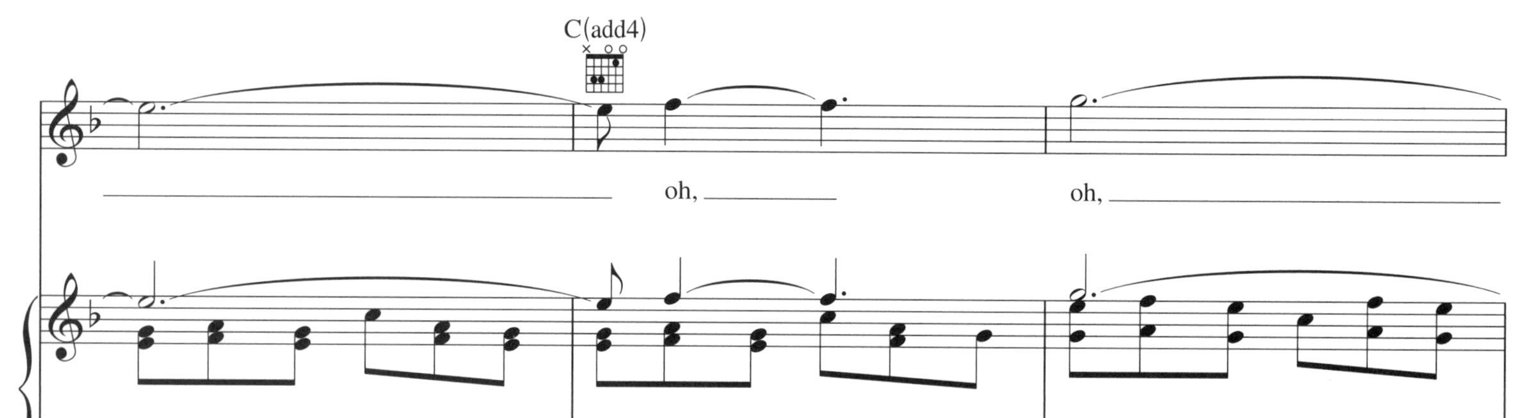
C(add4)
oh,
oh,

F5
oh.

TELL ME A STORY

Words and Music by PHILLIP PHILLIPS
and DAVID RYAN HARRIS

Fm11
6fr
So don't be - lieve in ev - 'ry - thing you see, be - cause
E♭/G
3fr
what you want might not be what you need. Hold your breath, jump with
E♭
3fr
E♭sus
6fr
me and we'll sur - vive. 'Cause
E♭
3fr
A♭maj9
3fr
Gm/A♭
3fr
E♭/A♭
6fr
B♭(add4)
you are the
sun that
moon that
Cm11

A♭(add2)
B♭/A♭
leads me to the light.
pulls me through the night.
A♭maj9
A♭6/9
Hope is just a
B♭(add4)
Cm11
E♭(add4)
ray of what ev-'ry-one should see.
A-lone is the
E♭/B♭
Fm11
E♭
B♭(add4)
street where you found me.
Scared of what's

A♭6/9
B♭(add4)
Cm11
E♭(add4)
be - hind you and scared of what's in front. ____ Live with what
To Coda
E♭/B♭
Fm11
E♭maj7
E♭/B♭
you have now, and make the best of what's to come.

E♭/A♭

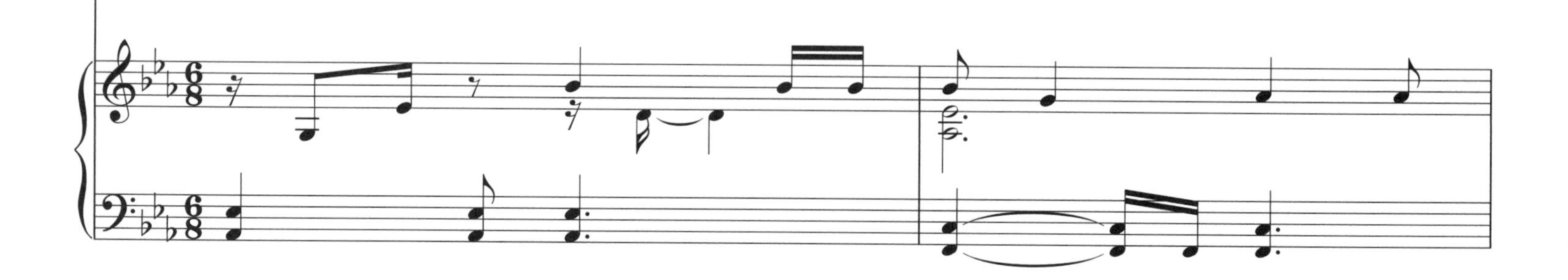
Fm11
Tell me a sto - ry long and

E♭/G
3fr
true. We aren't what we say; we are what we
E♭(add4)
do. Just piec - es of a puz - zle
E♭
3fr
E♭sus2
6fr
A♭(add2)
4fr
to find where we stand, just con - fused.
B♭/A♭
D.S. al Coda
So
CODA
E♭maj7
3fr
E♭/B♭
6fr
come.

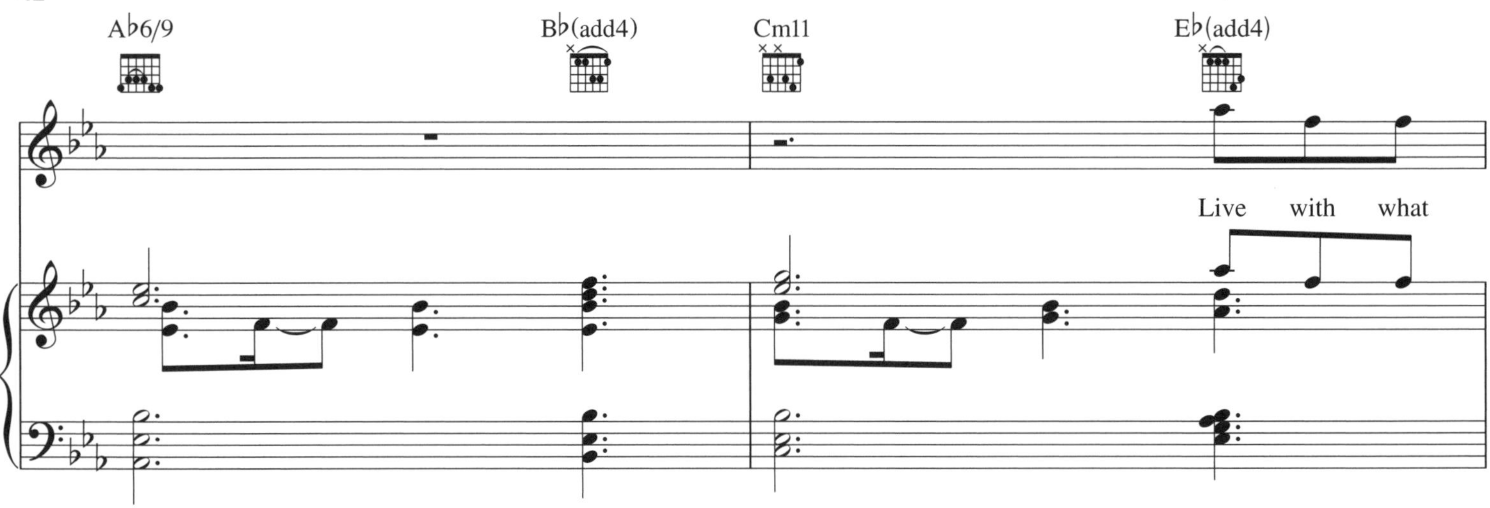
A♭6/9
B♭(add4)
Cm11
E♭(add4)
Live with what

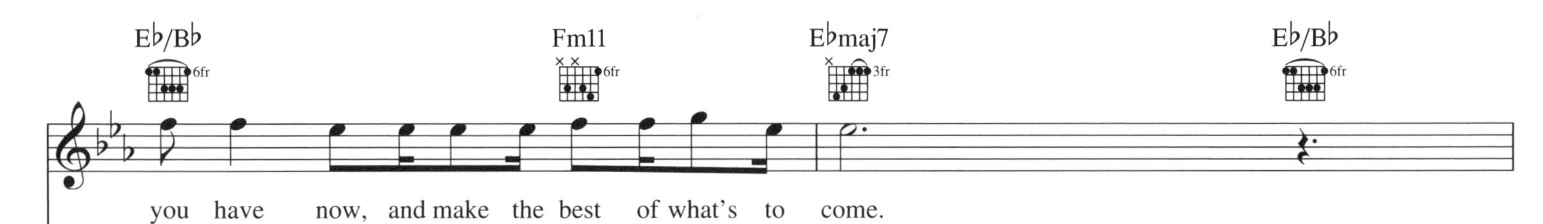
E♭/B♭
Fm11
E♭maj7
E♭/B♭
you have now, and make the best of what's to come.

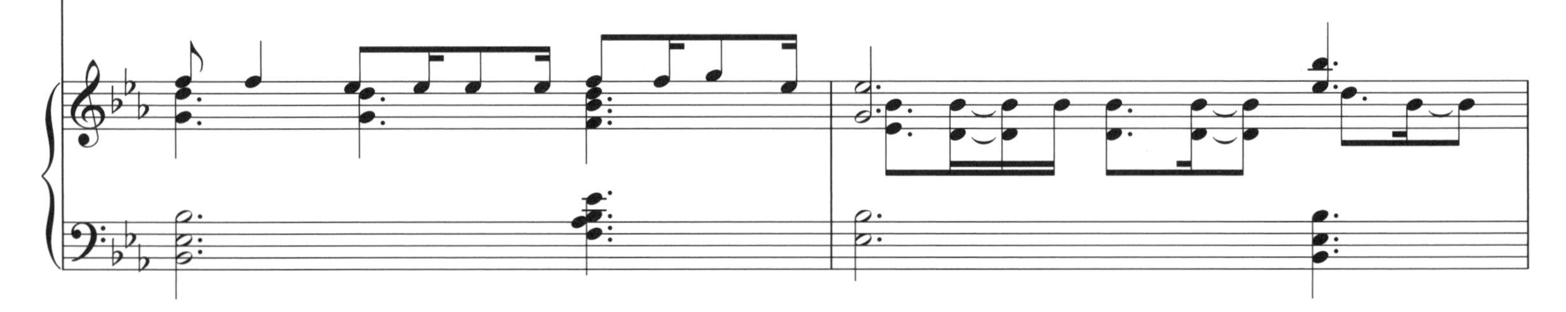

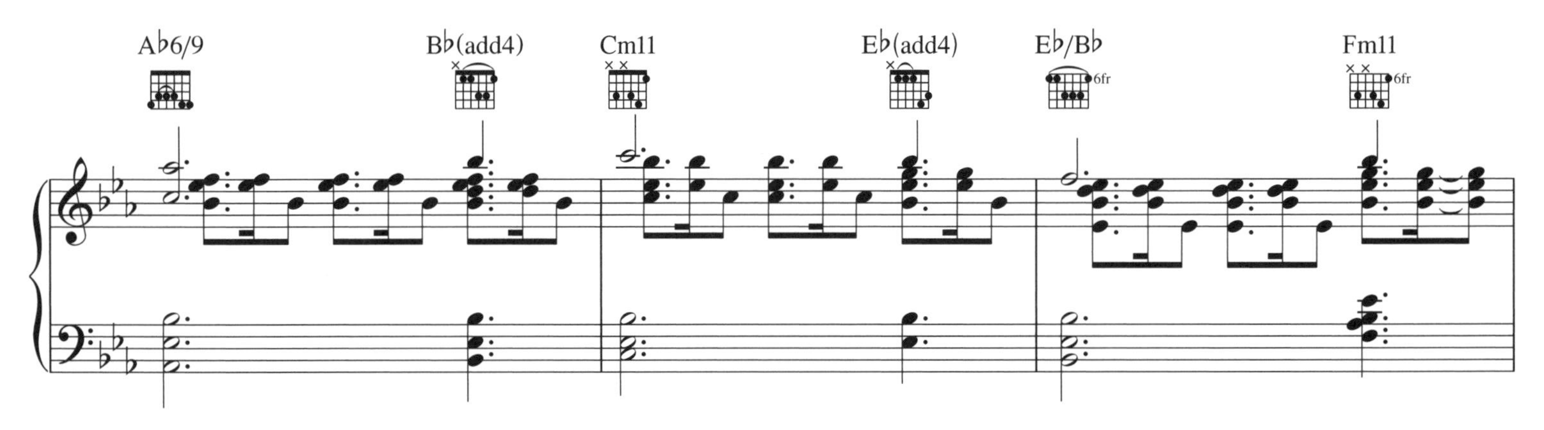
A♭6/9
B♭(add4)
Cm11
E♭(add4)
E♭/B♭
Fm11

E♭maj7
E♭/B♭
A♭6/9
B♭(add4)
Hope is just a ray of what ev-'ry - one should

Cm11
Eb(add4)
Eb/Bb
6fr
Fm11
6fr
see. A - lone is the street where you found
Eb
3fr
Bb(add4)
Ab6/9
Bb(add4)
me. Scared of what's be - hind you and scared of what's
Cm11
Eb(add4)
Eb/Bb
6fr
Fm11
6fr
in front. Live with what you have now, and make the best of what's to
Ebmaj7
3fr
Eb/Bb
6fr
Gm7/Ab
come.

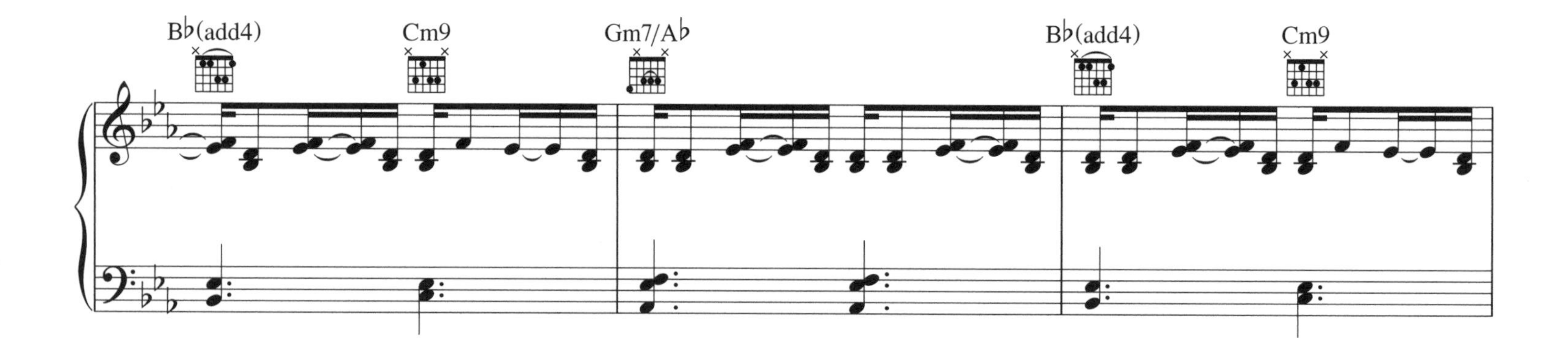
B♭(add4)
Cm9
Gm7/A♭
B♭(add4)
Cm9

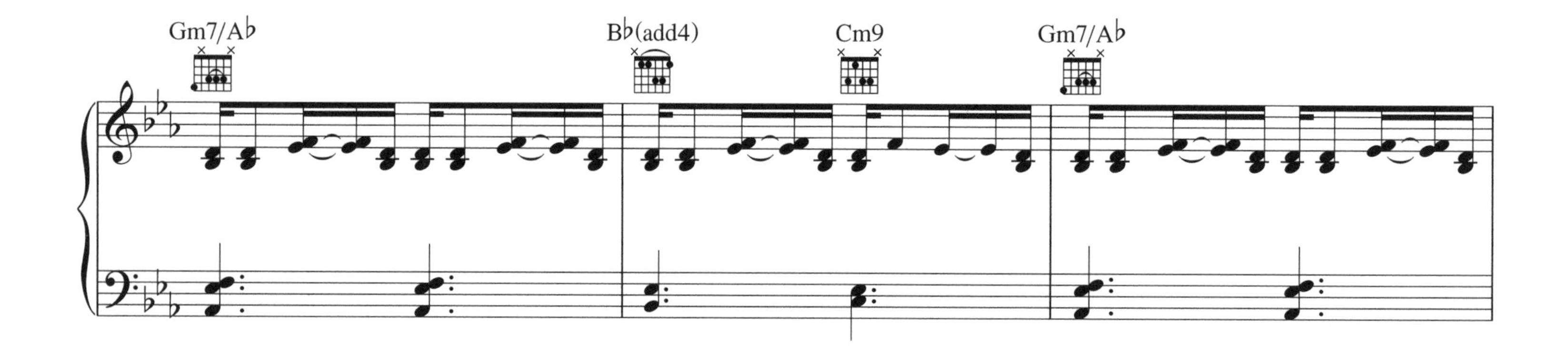
Gm7/A♭
B♭(add4)
Cm9
Gm7/A♭

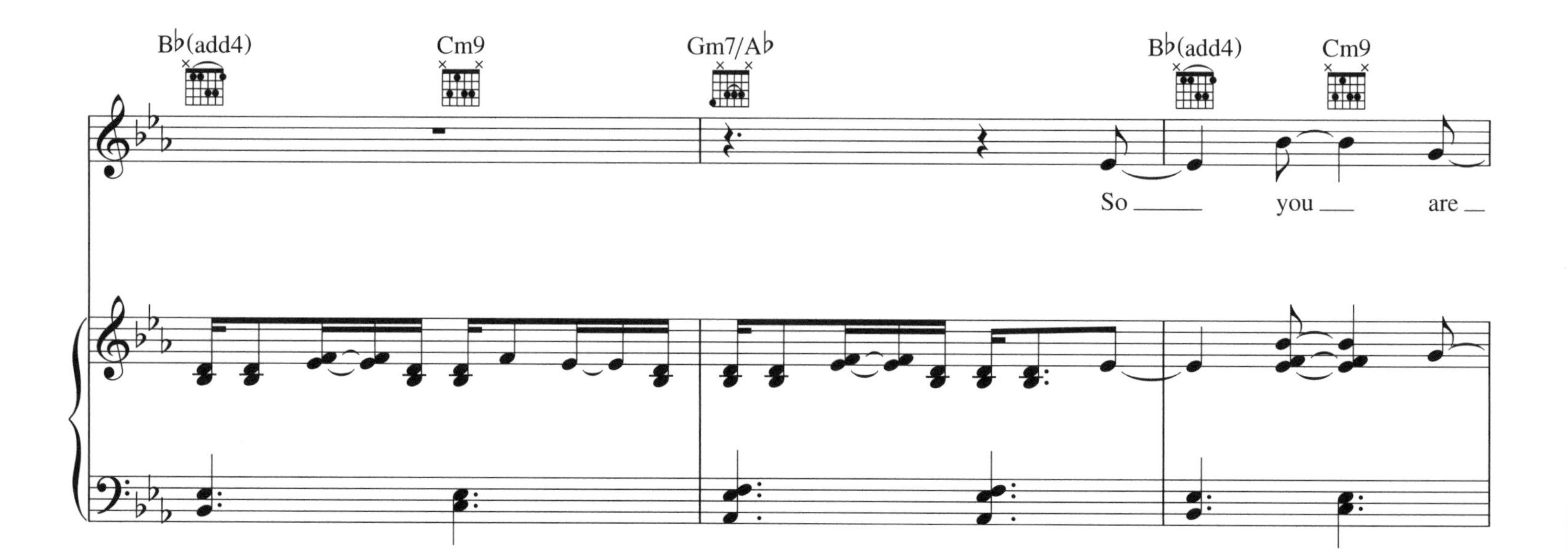
B♭(add4)
Cm9
Gm7/A♭
B♭(add4)
Cm9
So you are

Gm7/A♭
B♭(add4)
Cm9
Gm7/A♭
the sun that leads me;
B♭(add4)
Cm9
Gm7/A♭
B♭(add4)
Cm9
you are the moon that
Gm7/A♭
B♭(add4)
Cm9
pulls me; you are
Gm7/A♭
B♭(add4)
Cm9
the light that

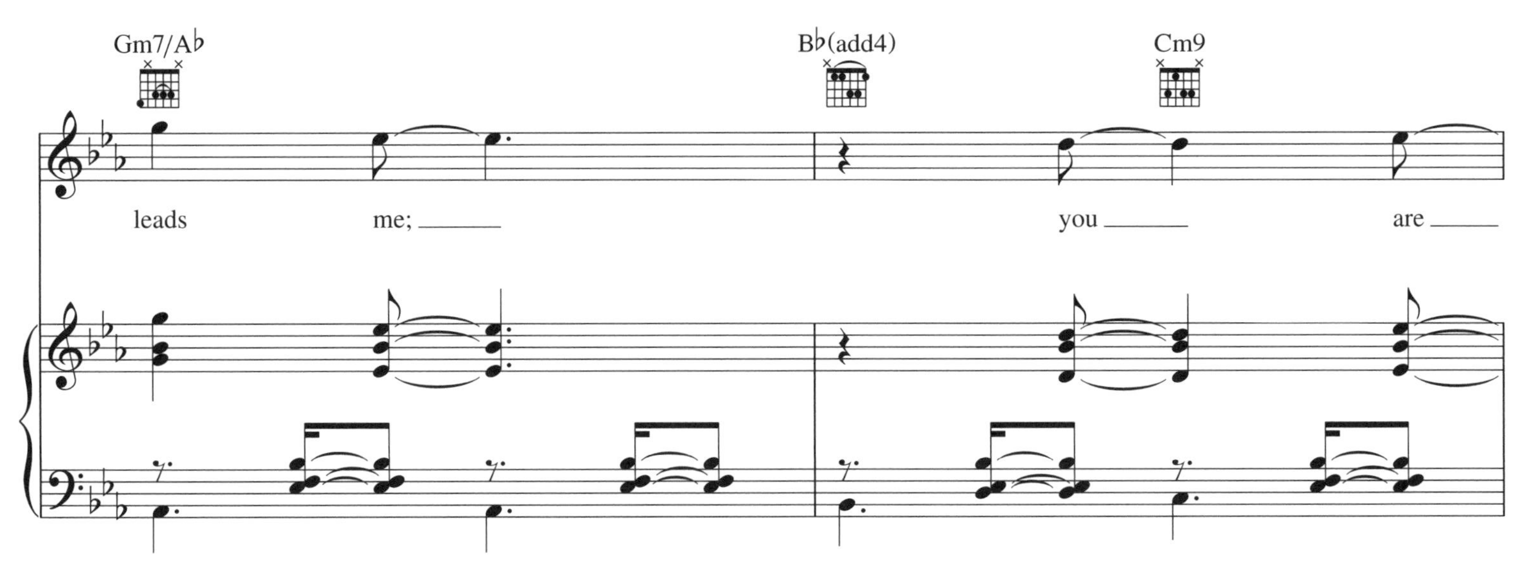
Gm7/A♭
B♭(add4)
Cm9
leads me;
you are

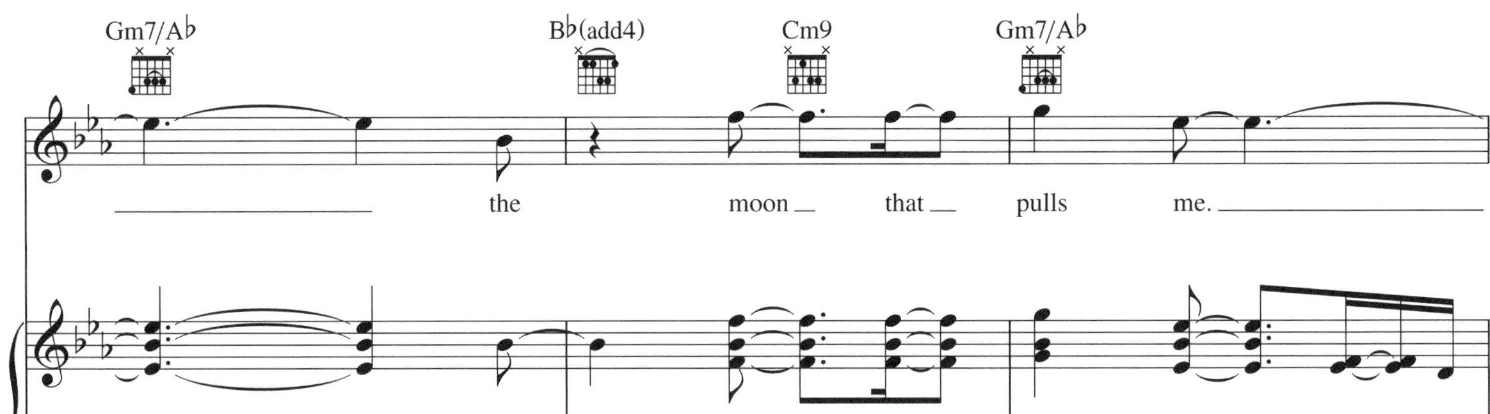
Gm7/A♭
B♭(add4)
Cm9
Gm7/A♭
the moon that pulls me.

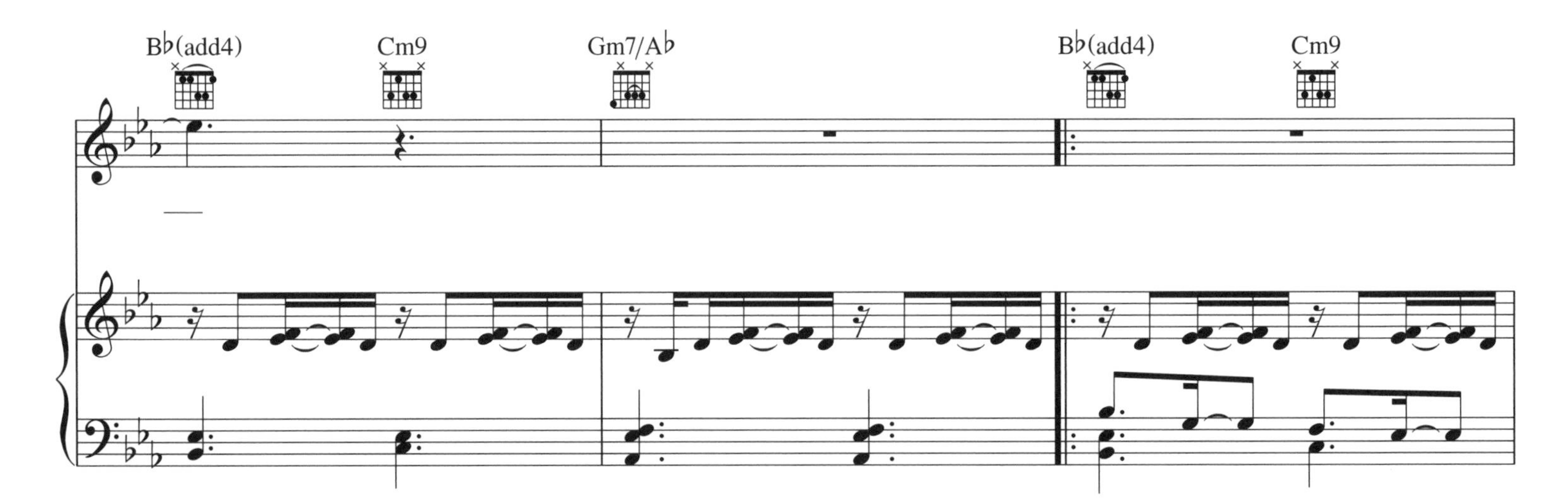
B♭(add4)
Cm9
Gm7/A♭
B♭(add4)
Cm9

Gm7/A♭
Repeat and Fade
B♭(add4)
Cm9
Gm7/A♭

GET UP GET DOWN

Words and Music by PHILLIP PHILLIPS,
GREGG WATTENBERG and DEREK FUHRMANN

Fmaj7
G
A5
5fr
Esus
A/D
Find out what's there, what you can be.
Bm7
A5
5fr
Dmaj7
Yes - ter - day was our time to turn back a - gain; in -
A5
5fr
Esus
A/D
stead we went through the fire to get lost in sin.
A5
5fr
Esus
A/D
3
Burn, ba - by, burn; let me cool you down a - gain.
3

A5
Esus
A/D
Turn, ba - by, turn to see where it all be - gins. 'Cause
F♯m
Dmaj9
A
C♯m7
it's al - right, it's out there. Go and get lost, girl.
F♯m
Dmaj9
A
N.C.
It's al - right, I'm out there. Let me take con - trol.
Am
Fmaj7
Get up, get down, move a lit - tle bit clos - er to the scene.

G
D
Find out what's there, something new to con - ceive there.
Am
F♯m7♭5
4fr
Get up, get down, get a lit - tle bit clos - er to me.
Fmaj7
To Coda
G5
3fr
E/G♯
Find out what's there, what you can be.
A
A/E
Dmaj9
4fr
Bm7

A
Dmaj9
4fr
Walk it off, but keep it on. Let it take con-trol of
ev-'ry cell in-side your bod-y, each and ev-'ry bone.
Burn, ba-by, burn, let's cool it down a-gain.
Turn, ba-by, turn to see where it all be-gins, yeah.
3
D.S. al Coda

CODA
Gsus2
Am
there, what you can be. Na, na, na, na, na,
F
G
D
no, na, na, na, na, na, no, na, na, na, na, na, no.
Am
F♯m7♭5
4fr
Get up, get down, just a lit-tle bit. Get up, get down. just a lit-tle bit.
Fmaj7
G
Get up, get down; let's get lost in this mer-ry go 'round and 'round.

Am7
F
Na, na, na, na, na, no, na, na, na, na, na,
G
D7(add4)
5fr
no, na, na, na, na, na, no.
Am7
F♯m7♭5
4fr
Get up, get down just a lit - tle bit. Get up, get down just a lit - tle bit.
Fmaj7
G
Get up, get down, find out what's there, find out if it's you and me.
3
3

Am
Fmaj7
Get up, get down, move a lit - tle bit clos - er to the scene.
G
D
Find out what's there, some-thing new to con - ceive there.
Am
F♯m7♭5
4fr
1
Fmaj7
Get up, get down, get a lit-tle bit clos - er to me.
Find out what's
G5
3fr
2
Fmaj7
G5
3fr
E/G♯
there, what you can be.
Find out what's there, what you can be.

WHERE WE CAME FROM

Words and Music by PHILLIP PHILLIPS
and JONATHAN GREEN

Dsus/C
Am7
Dsus/C
we said in an - ger still ech - o in my brain.

D6
Em7
A - lone through the dark - ness in this cave
the stars to build a map to you.

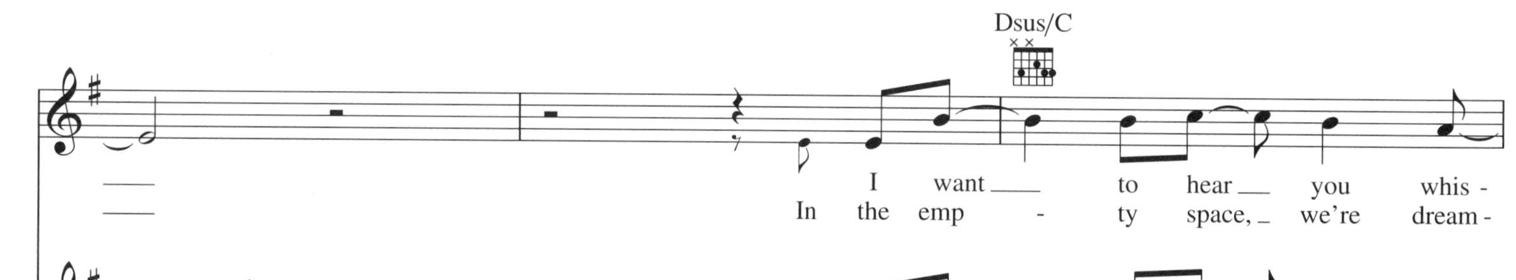
Dsus/C
I want to hear you whis -
In the emp - ty space, we're dream -

Am7
Dsus/C
D
- per, hang on ev - 'ry word you say.
- ing, but we still know the truth.

Em
C
Bm
Climb the moun - tain, swim for
D
Em
Cmaj7
shore. Bring it back to how it
Bm
D
C(add2)
was be - fore. Take it out. Blow it up.
G
D
Em7
Ig - nite the mem - o - ry in be - tween us. Through the storm

C(add2)
Gmaj7
D(add2)
D
and all the dust,
tak - ing out
these walls with a
Em7
C(add2)
D(add4)
3fr
can - non - ball.
But don't let it go, don't
Em
D(add4)
C(add2)
D(add4)
give up the ghost.
We're all star - ing at the
3
To Coda
1
moon and the sun,
just try - ing to re - mem - ber where we came

Em7
from.
I con - nect
2
C6/9
Dsus
mem - ber where we came
from.
(Oh,
Em11
G6/9
C6/9
D6/9
5fr
4fr
oh.)
Em11
C6/9
Dsus
5fr
(Oh,

Em11
5fr
G6/9
C6/9
oh.)
Am11
3fr
C6/9
D(add4)
3fr
Em
So climb the
C
B5
D5
5fr
moun - tain,
swim for shore.
Em
C
B5
Bring it back to what it was be - fore.

D5
5fr
D.S. al Coda
Take it out.
CODA
C(add2)
mem - ber where we came from.
G
D(add4)
3fr
Just try - ing to re - mem - ber where we came
C(add2)
G
D(add4)
3fr
from.
C(add2)
D(add4)
3fr
Em
D(add4)
3fr
But don't let it go, don't give up the ghost

C(add2)
D(add4)
3fr
We're all star - ing at the moon and the sun,
just try - ing to re - mem - ber where we came from.
Em7
Csus2
3fr
Em
D(add4)
3fr
C
Gmaj7/B
Em

DRIVE ME

Words and Music by PHILLIP PHILLIPS
and BEN NEIL

F♯m E Bm7 C♯m7 A5 G♯5
4fr 5fr 4fr
then I hear, ah, ooh, like
F♯m E F♯m E
grav - i - ty pul - ling me in. I'm sink - ing in this space with - in.
Bm7 C♯m7 A5 G♯5
4fr 5fr 4fr
I can't help but giv - ing in to this
F♯m E F♯m E
stran - ger with no name, danc - ing like a flame,

Bm7
C♯m7
4fr
A5
5fr
G♯5
4fr
like a moth that can - not be turned a - way.

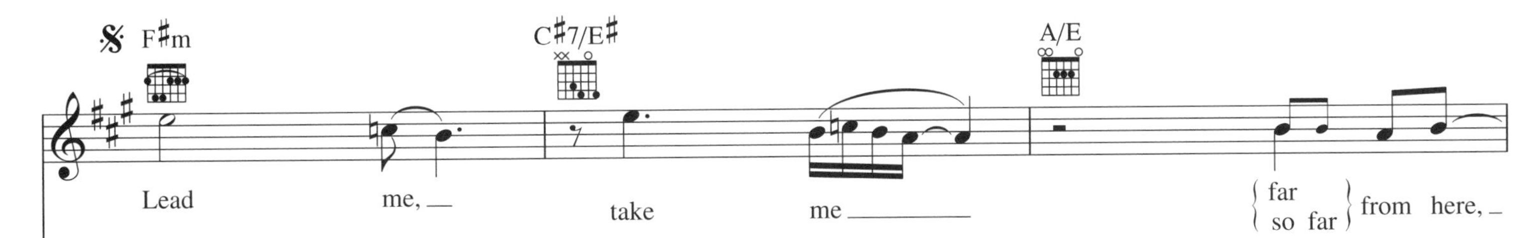
F♯m
C♯7/E♯
A/E
Lead me, take me
far
so far
from here,

D♯m7♭5
6fr
D
C♯7♯9
3fr
sweet - ly. Do

F♯m
Dmaj7
what you do, and do what you will, let me get down, take a hold of the wheel.

C♯7
Bm/A
Bsus(add2)
G♯sus
4fr
Asus2
Let me drive you crazy. Do
F♯m
Dmaj7
what you do and do what you will. Let me get down;
I'll be the drug you
I'll be all that you
C♯7
To Coda
Esus
Bsus2
feel. I'll let you drive me cra - zy.
F♯(add4)
E
F♯(add4)
E
I love your moves,

F♯m
E
F♯m
E
I like your style. With them hips you drive me wild. I'm the
Bm7
C♯m7
4fr
A5
5fr
G♯5
4fr
pup - pet to your strings; you keep on mov - ing me. In a world
F♯m
E
F♯m
E
you keep on turn - ing, turn - ing for me now.
Bm7
C♯m7
4fr
A5
5fr
G♯5
4fr
Ev - 'ry - thing we have is mov - ing down, down, down. We

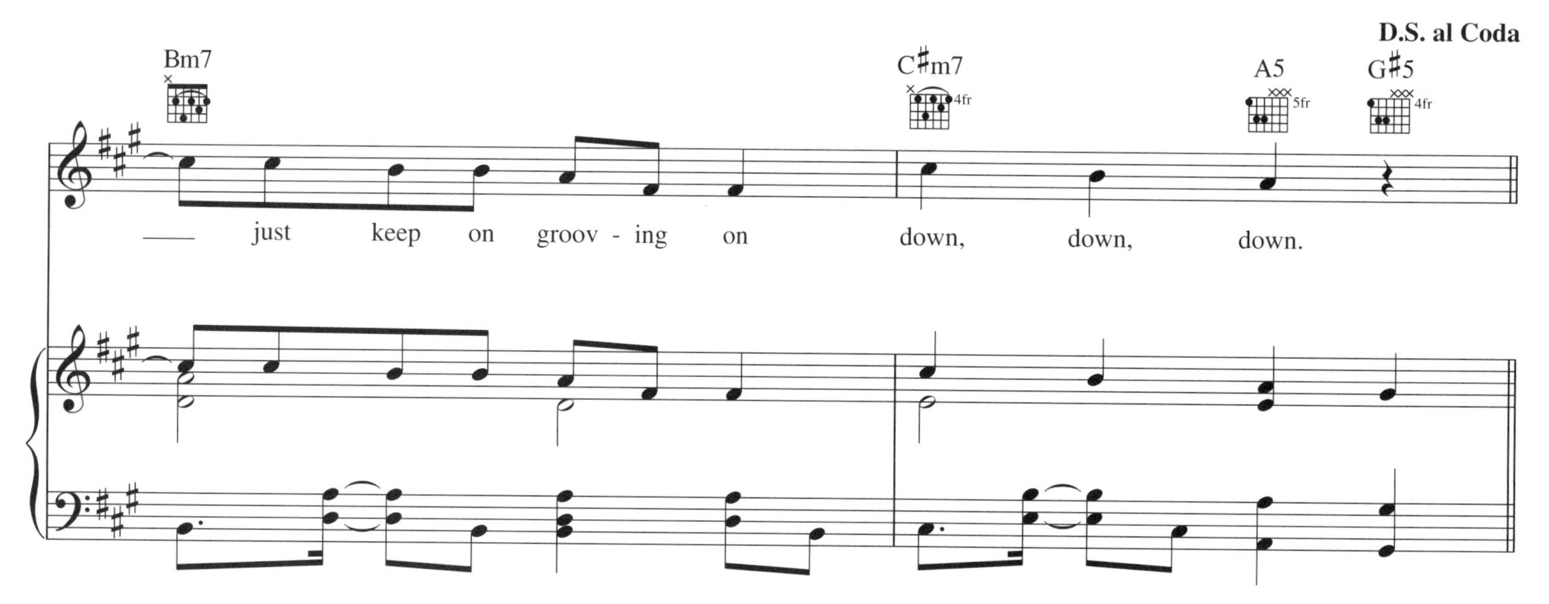
D.S. al Coda
Bm7
C♯m7
4fr
A5
5fr
G♯5
4fr
just keep on groov - ing on down, down, down.

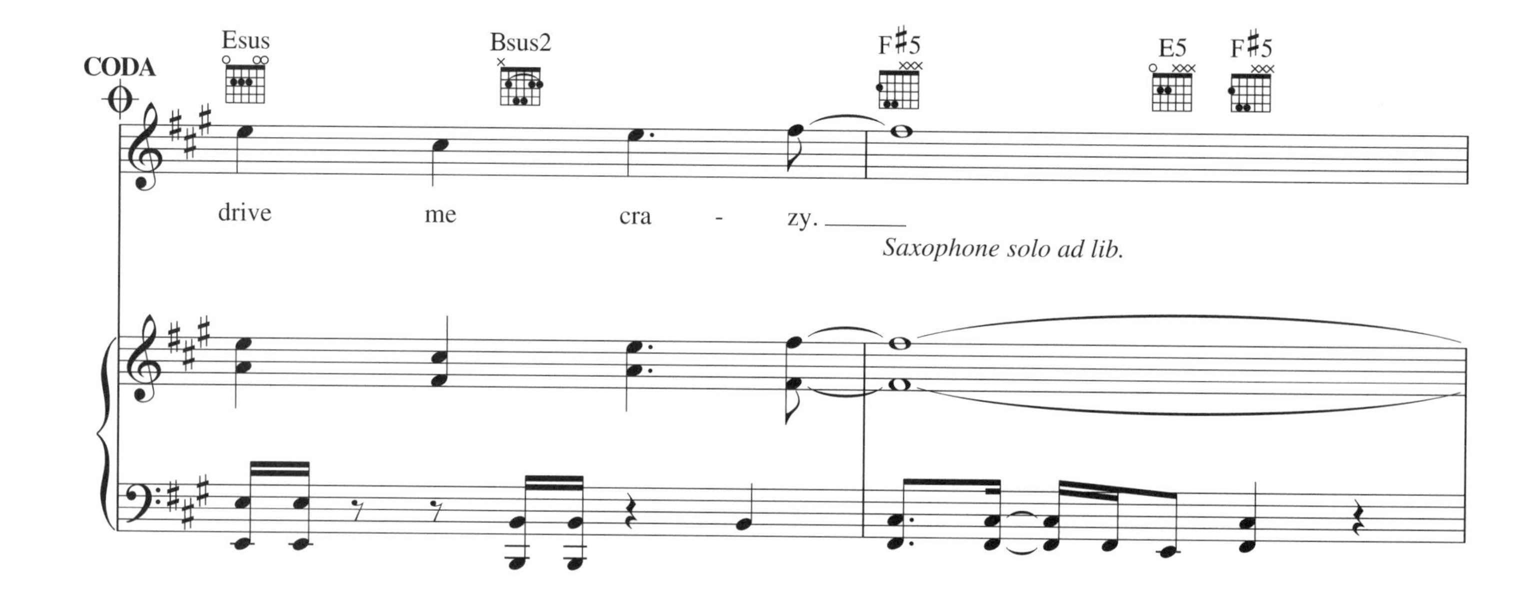
CODA
Esus
Bsus2
F♯5
E5
F♯5
drive me cra - zy.
Saxophone solo ad lib.

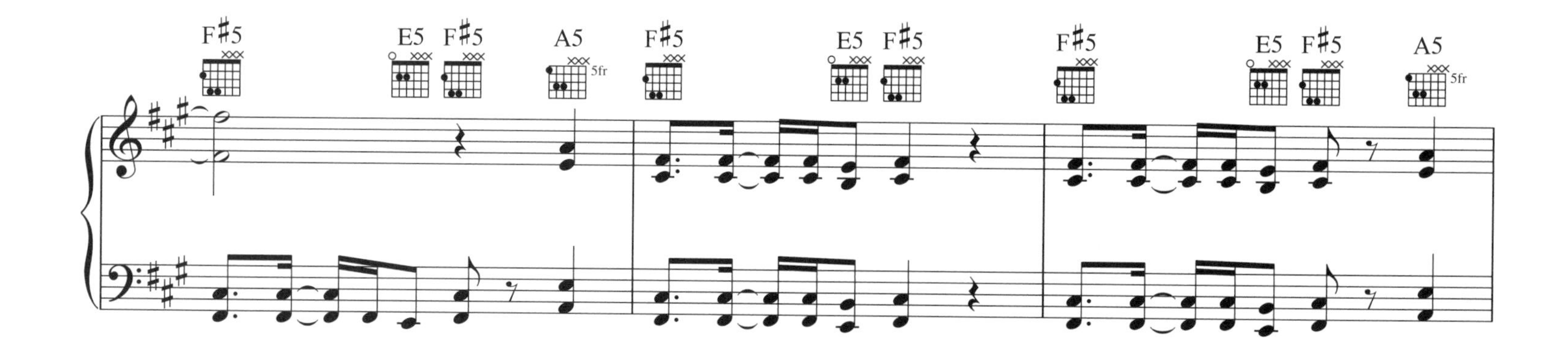
F♯5
E5
F♯5
A5
5fr
F♯5
E5
F♯5
F♯5
E5
F♯5
A5
5fr

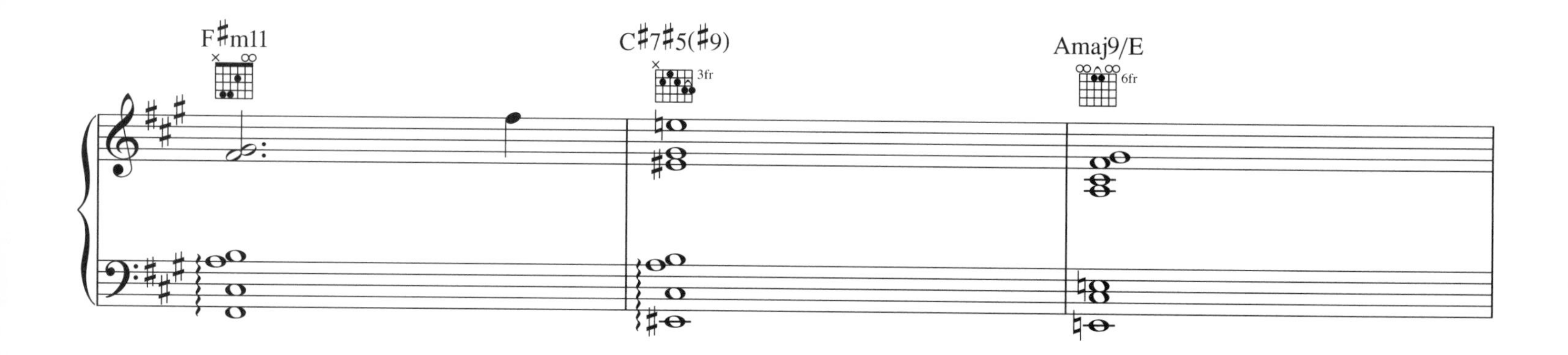
F♯m11
C♯7♯5(♯9)
3fr
Amaj9/E
6fr

B9/D♯
F♯m7(add4)
C♯7/E♯

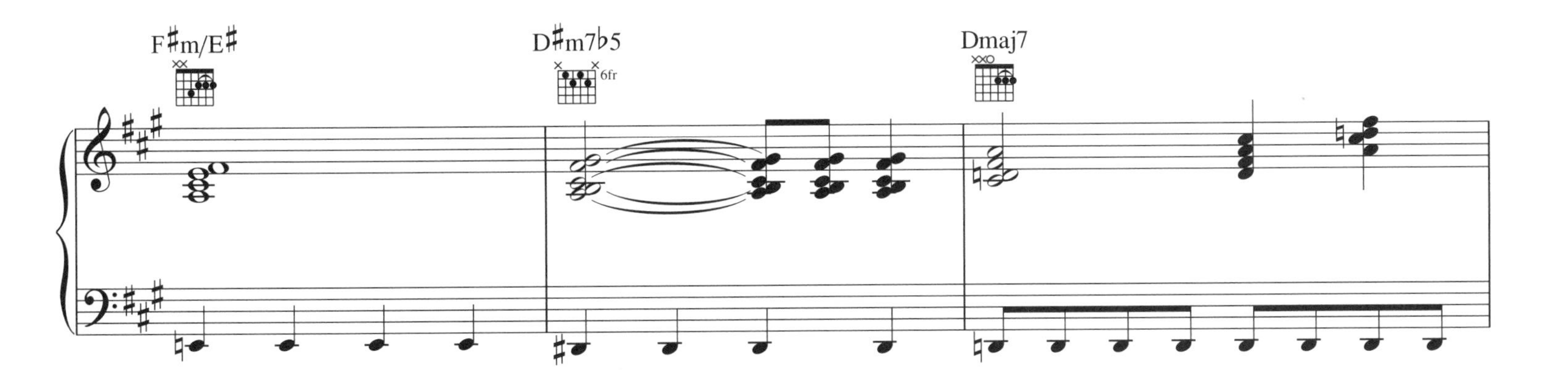
F♯m/E♯
D♯m7♭5
6fr
Dmaj7

C♯7♯9
3fr
F♯m
(Solo ends)
Do what you do, and do what you will, let

Dmaj7
C♯7
me get down, take a hold of the wheel. Ba - by, let me

Bm/A
Bsus(add2)
G♯sus
4fr
Asus2
F♯m
drive you cra - zy.
Do what you do and do what you will.
1
Dmaj7
C♯7
Let me get down; I'll be all that you feel.
I'll let you
Esus
Bsus2
drive me.
2
Dmaj7
Do
Let me get down; I'll be all that
C♯7
you feel.
I'll let you
Esus
Bsus2
drive me cra - zy,

F♯m
Dmaj7
hey, oh. Ba - by, say
C♯7
D/A
E/B
A/G♯
D/A
how. I'll let you drive me cra - zy. Oh,
F♯m
Dmaj7
oh, we're here now, say, oh, we're here now, get it all
C♯7
Esus
Bsus2
N.C.
out, I'll let you drive me cra - zy.

WANTED IS LOVE

Words and Music by
PHILLIP PHILLIPS

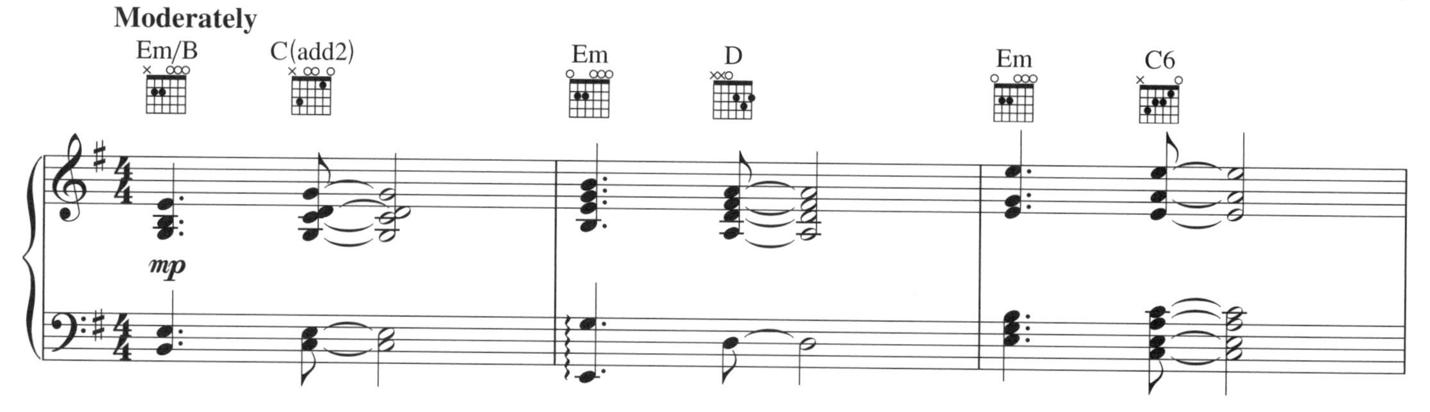

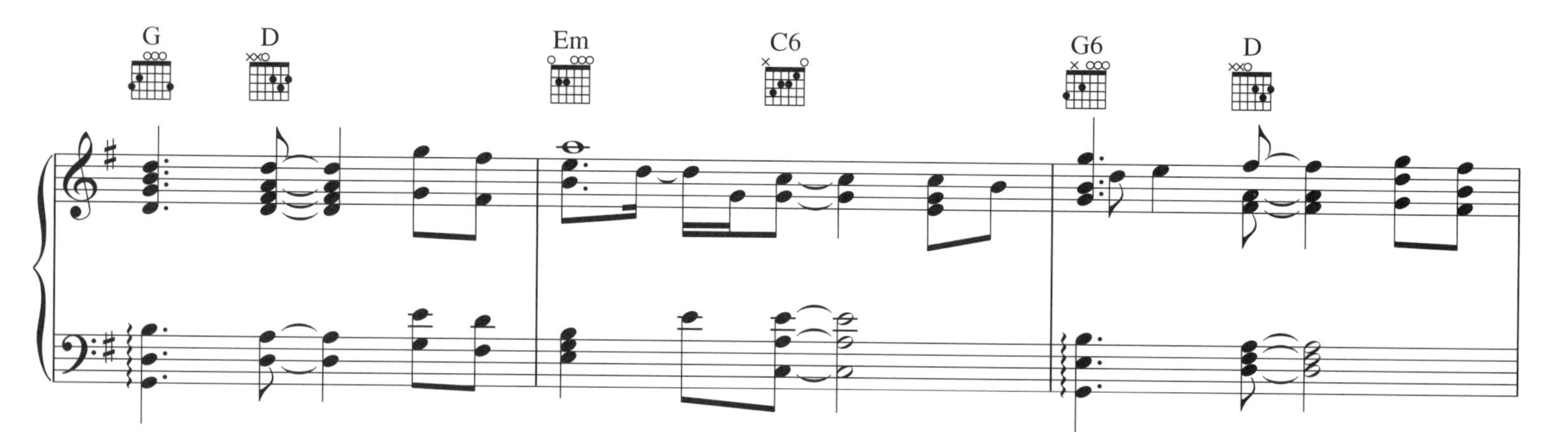

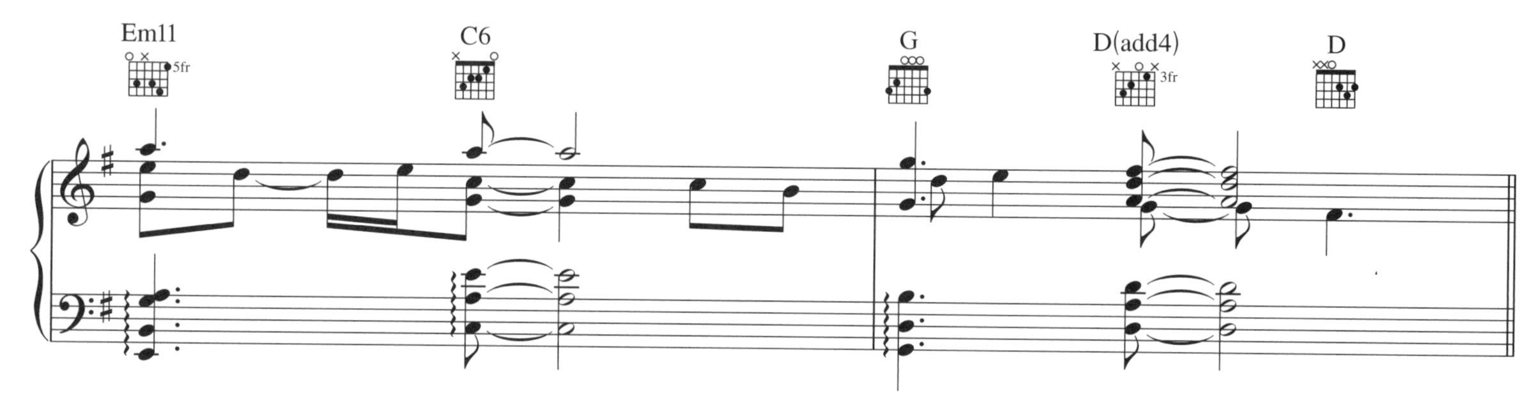

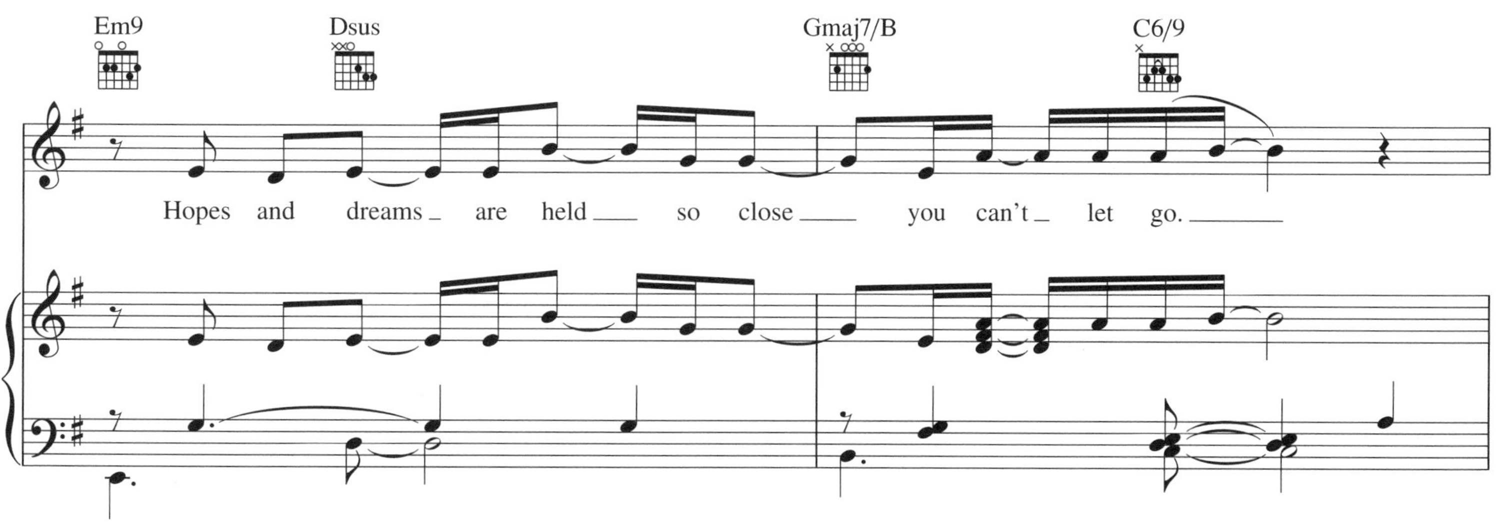
Em9
Dsus
Gmaj7/B
C6/9
Hopes and dreams are held so close you can't let go.

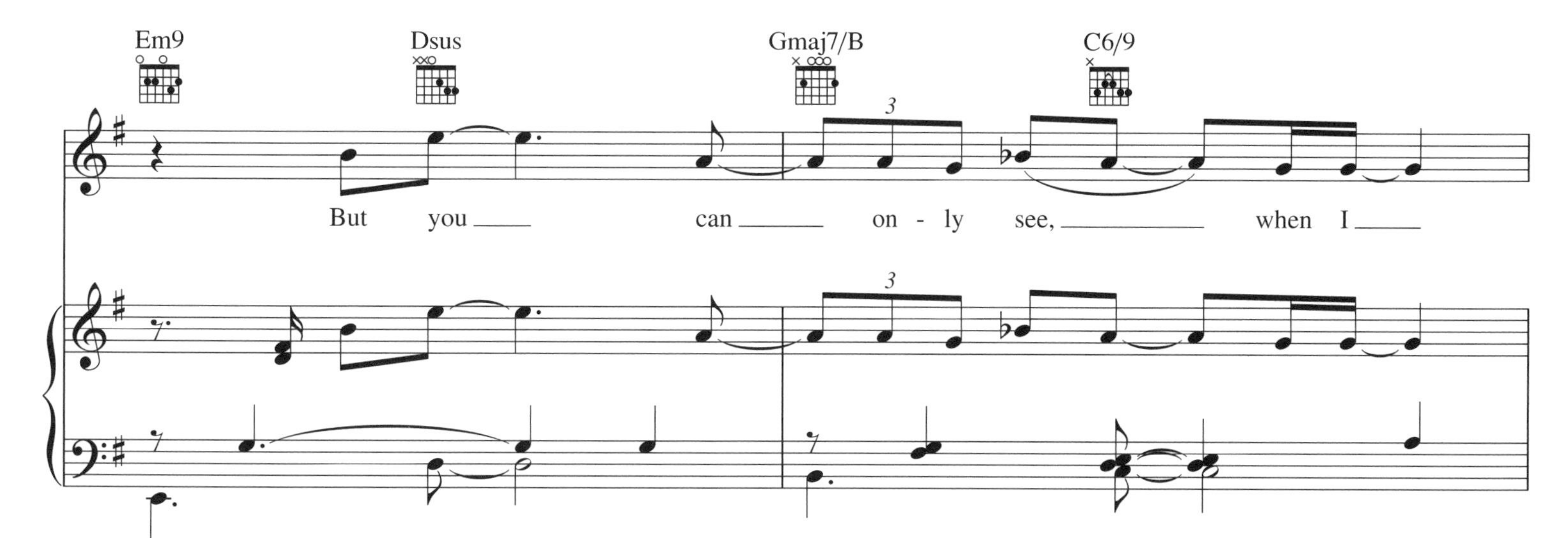
Em9
Dsus
Gmaj7/B
C6/9
3
But you can on - ly see, when I
3

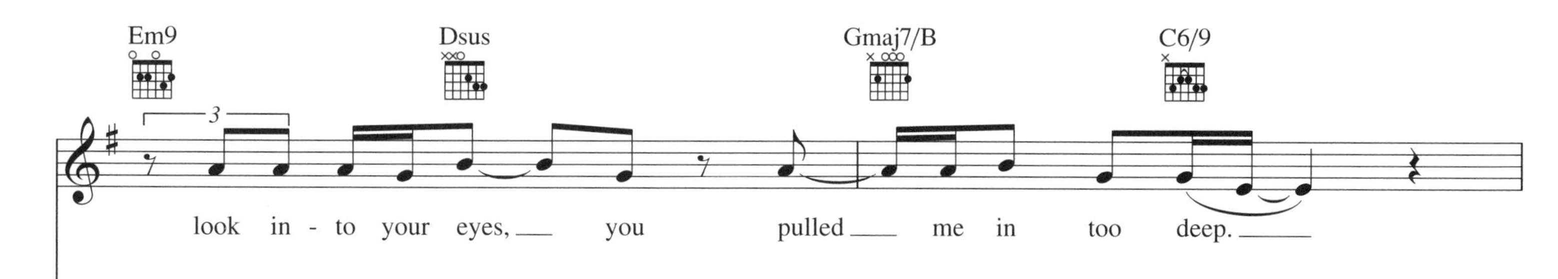
Em9
Dsus
Gmaj7/B
C6/9
3
look in - to your eyes, you pulled me in too deep.

3

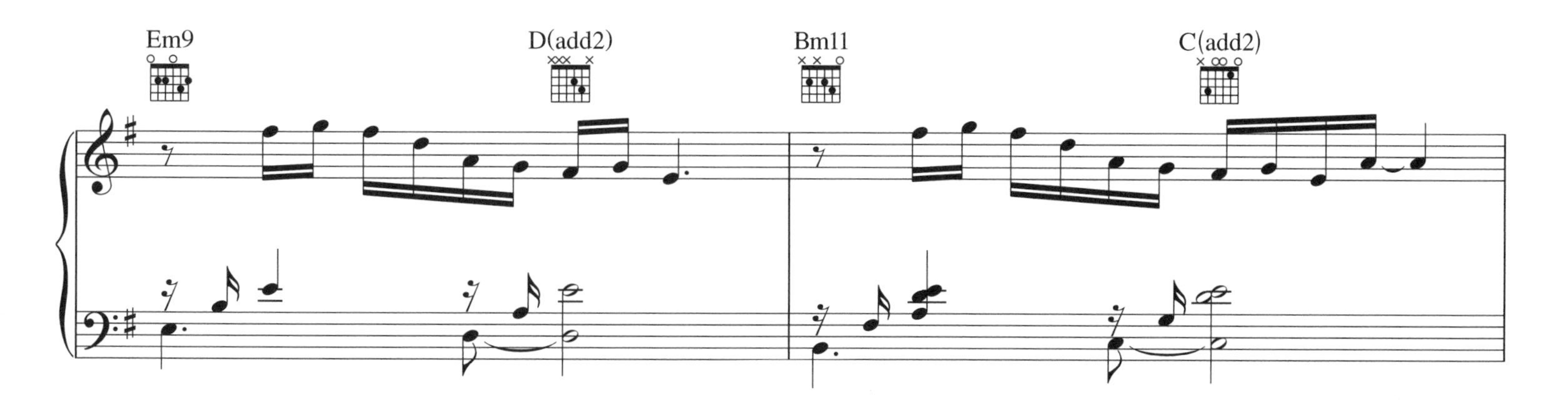
Em9
D(add2)
Bm11
C(add2)

Em9
Dsus
Gmaj7/B
C(add2)
Take me in, take me out, till I'm
nothing more than words spoken from your sweet, sweet mouth.
And dance around like no one can see, baby.
Move your body with the rhythm, move your body next to me. Wanted is love,

Em7
C(add2)
G
D7/F♯
not go - ing in - sane.
You know you've got to
Em7
C(add2)
G
D7/F♯
hold on to what you love before it's gone a - way.
Want - ed is love,
Em7
C(add2)
G
D7/F♯
not go - ing in - sane.
You know you've got to
Em7
C(add2)
G
D7/F♯
hold on to what you love before it's gone a - way.
One

Em9 Dsus Gmaj7/B C(add2)
step to you and I'm sink-ing in your lies, on-ly to
Em9 Dsus Gmaj7/B C(add2)
see the truth hid-den be-hind your e-vil eyes.
Em9 Dsus Gmaj7/B C(add2)
And no light could lead me to the ways of you. Is it me,
Em9 Dsus Gmaj7/B C(add2)
or am I a-lone? It's all such mys-ter-y. Want-ed is love,

Em7
C(add2)
G
D7/F#
not go-ing in-sane.
You know you've got to
Em7
C(add2)
G
D7/F#
hold on to what you love be-fore it's gone a-way.
Want-ed is love,
Em7
C(add2)
G
D7/F#
not go-ing in-sane.
You know you've got to
Em7
C(add2)
G
D7/F#
hold on to what you love be-fore it's gone a-way.
Want-ed is
3
3

Em7
C(add2)
G
love.
Em7
C(add2)
G
D/F♯
Want-ed is love,
Em
C
C♯dim
C
4fr
not go-ing in-sane,
no.
You know you've got to
Em
C
C♯dim
C
4fr
seek ev-'ry-thing you love be-fore it's gone a-way.
Want-ed is
3

Em
C
C♯dim
4fr
C
love, not go-ing in-sane, no. You know you've got to
Em
C
C♯dim
4fr
C
seek ev-'ry-thing you lost be-fore it's gone a-way. Want-ed is
3
3
Em7
C(add2)
G
D/F♯
love.
Em7
C(add2)
G
D/F♯
Want-ed is
3
3

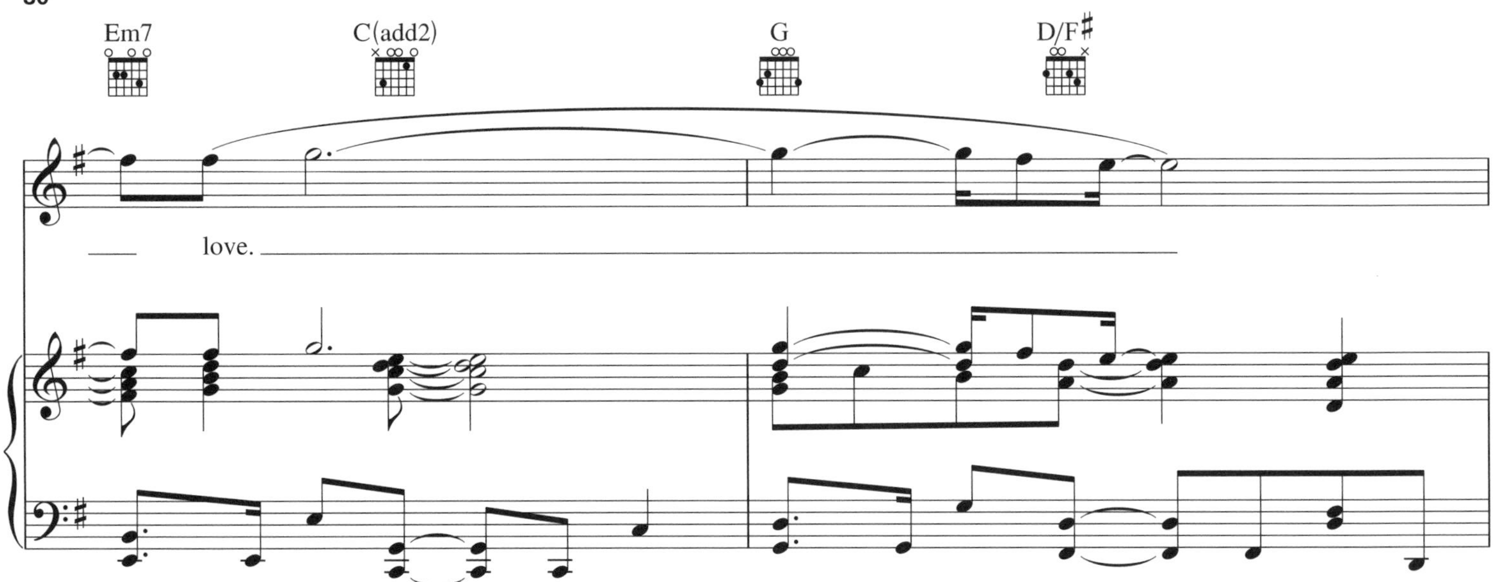
Em7
C(add2)
G
D/F♯
love.

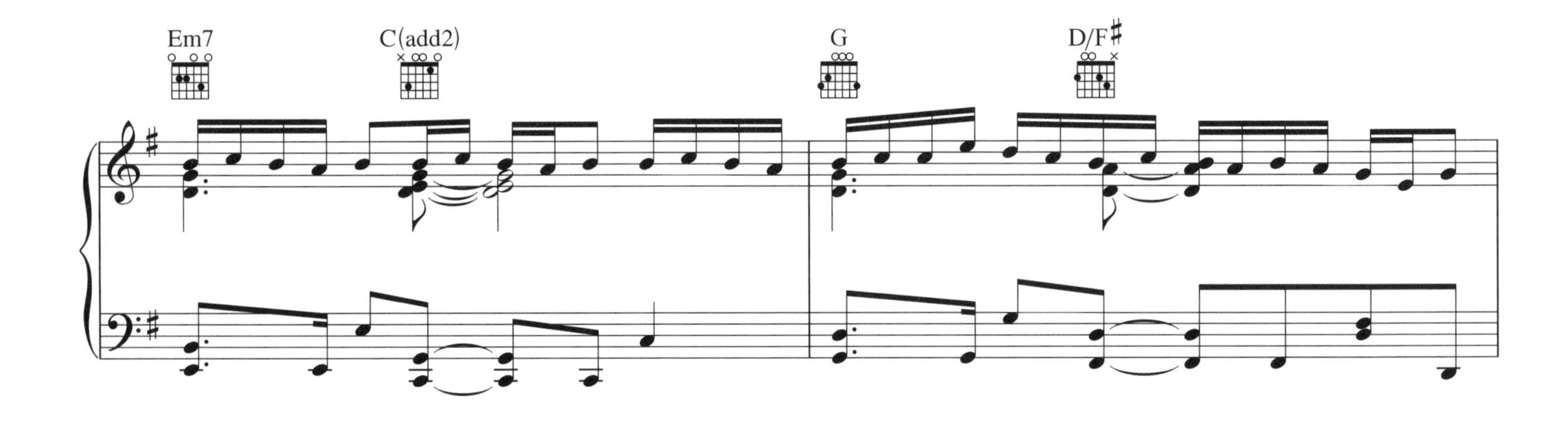
Em7
C(add2)
G
D/F♯

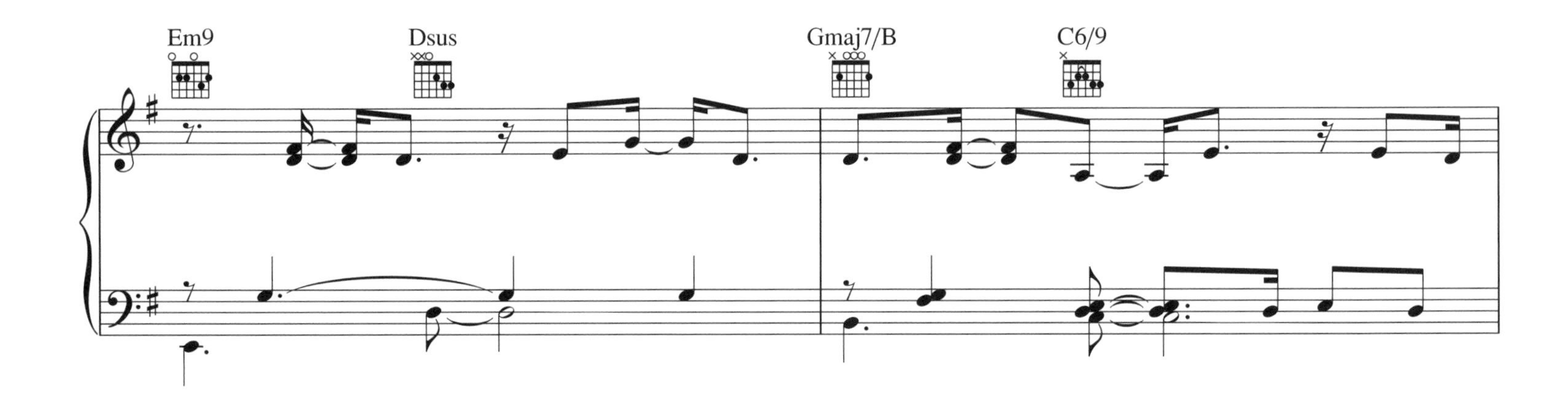
Em9
Dsus
Gmaj7/B
C6/9

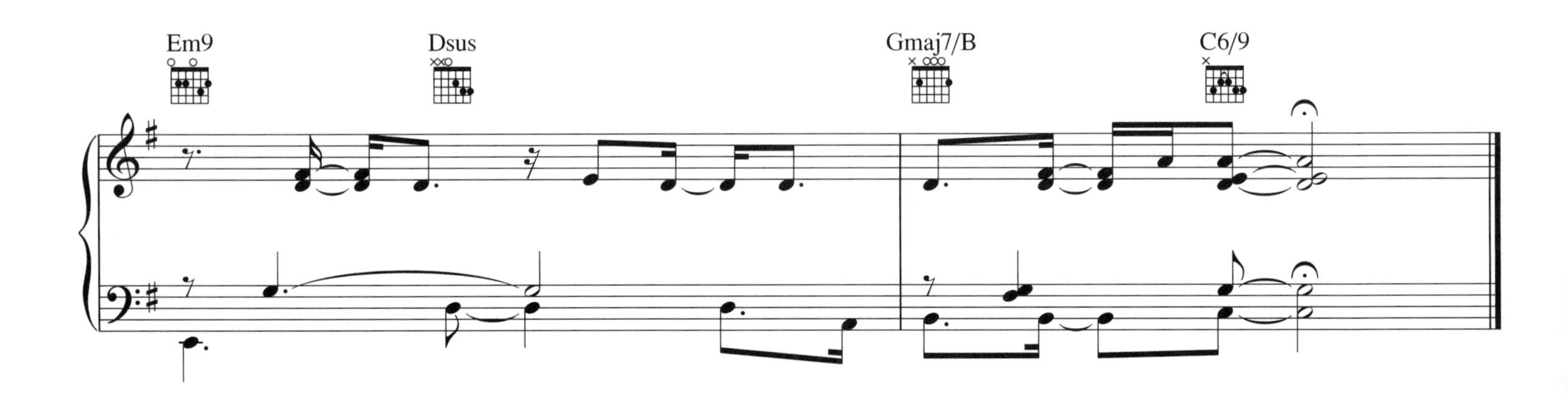
Em9
Dsus
Gmaj7/B
C6/9

CAN'T GO WRONG

Words and Music by PHILLIP PHILLIPS, GREG HOLDEN and DREW PEARSON

Moderately, in 2

Esus Asus2 Asus2/G♯

mf

F♯m7 Esus Asus2

I've seen the lights come from the flash-

Asus2/G♯ F♯m7 Esus

-es in the dark. I feel like a blind

Asus2 Asus2/G♯ F♯m7

man try - ing to make a start, and I don't

A5
5fr
F♯m
know,
no, I don't know

Esus
Asus2
where I'm gon - na go.

Asus2/G♯
F♯m7
Esus
I've seen the sun
Nev - er mind

Asus2
Asus2/G♯
F♯m7
come up a mile off the ground,
all the times that I just could - n't wait.

Esus
Asus2
Asus2/G♯
flew back the oth - er way, and saw it go back down.
I can't re-mem - ber when it all be-gan to change.
F♯m7
Esus
Asus2
I know the days change, but
Watch - ing the grass grow and
Asus2/G♯
F♯m7
Esus
al-ways seem the same. I'll take the best
die from sum-mer to fall, it's fun-ny how a
Asus2
Asus2/G♯
F♯m7
of what I can for my mis - takes. And now I
year pass - es by, and you don't no-tice at all. I

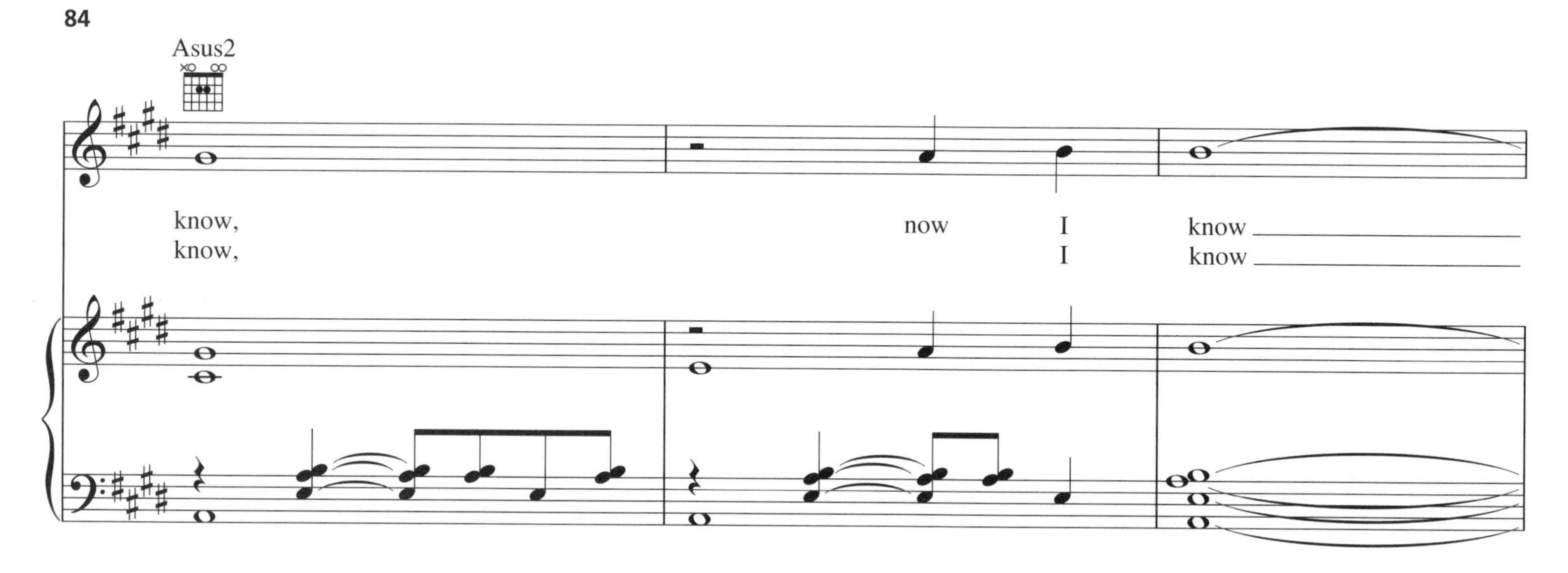
Asus2
know, now I know
know, I know

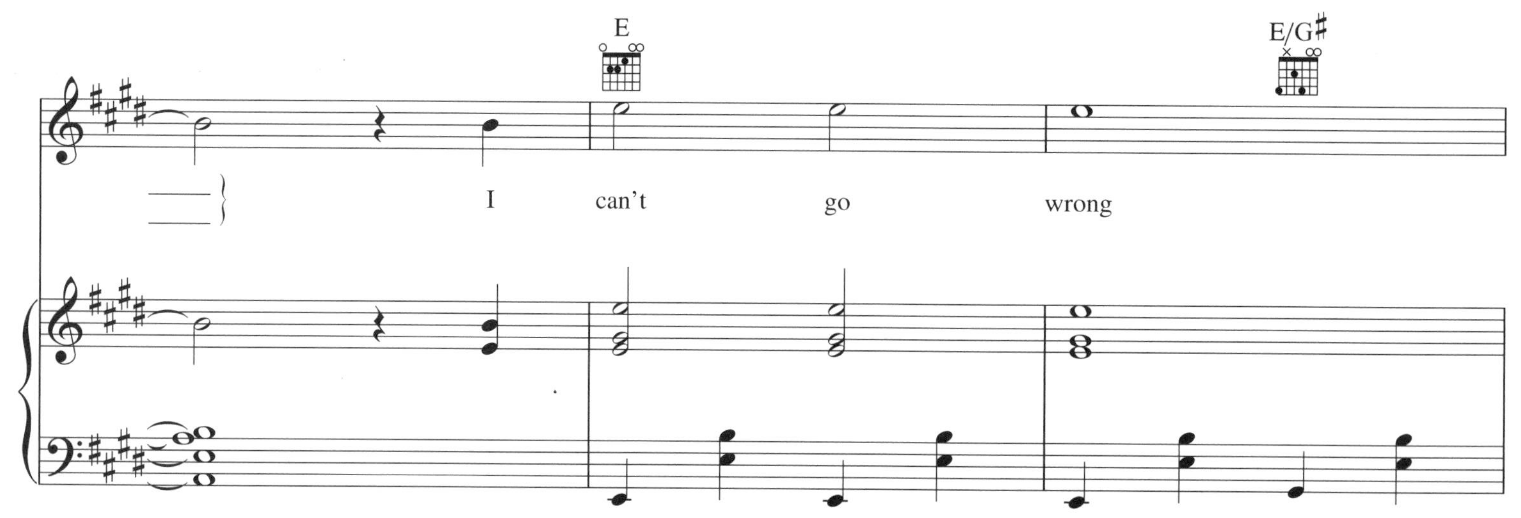
E
E/G♯
I can't go wrong

Asus2
C♯m7
4fr
as long as I re - mem - ber where I'm

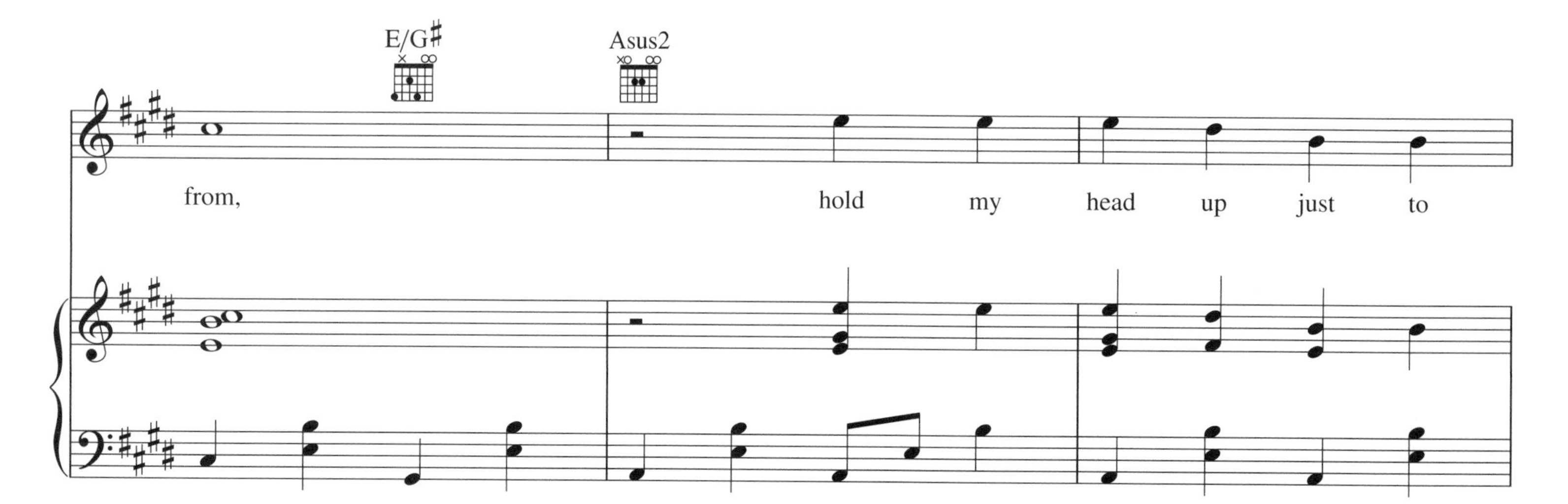
E/G♯
Asus2
from, hold my head up just to

E
E/G#
Asus2
keep it clear. I want a

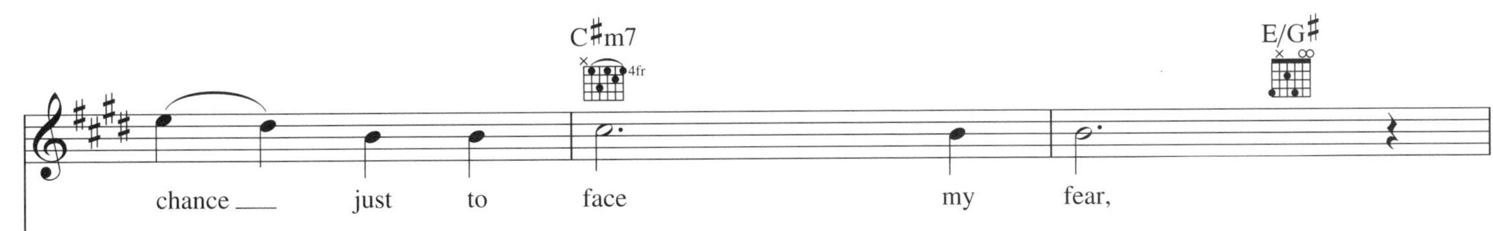
C#m7
4fr
E/G#
chance just to face my fear,

Asus2
1
Esus
face my fear. Oh.

Asus2
Asus2/G#
F#m7

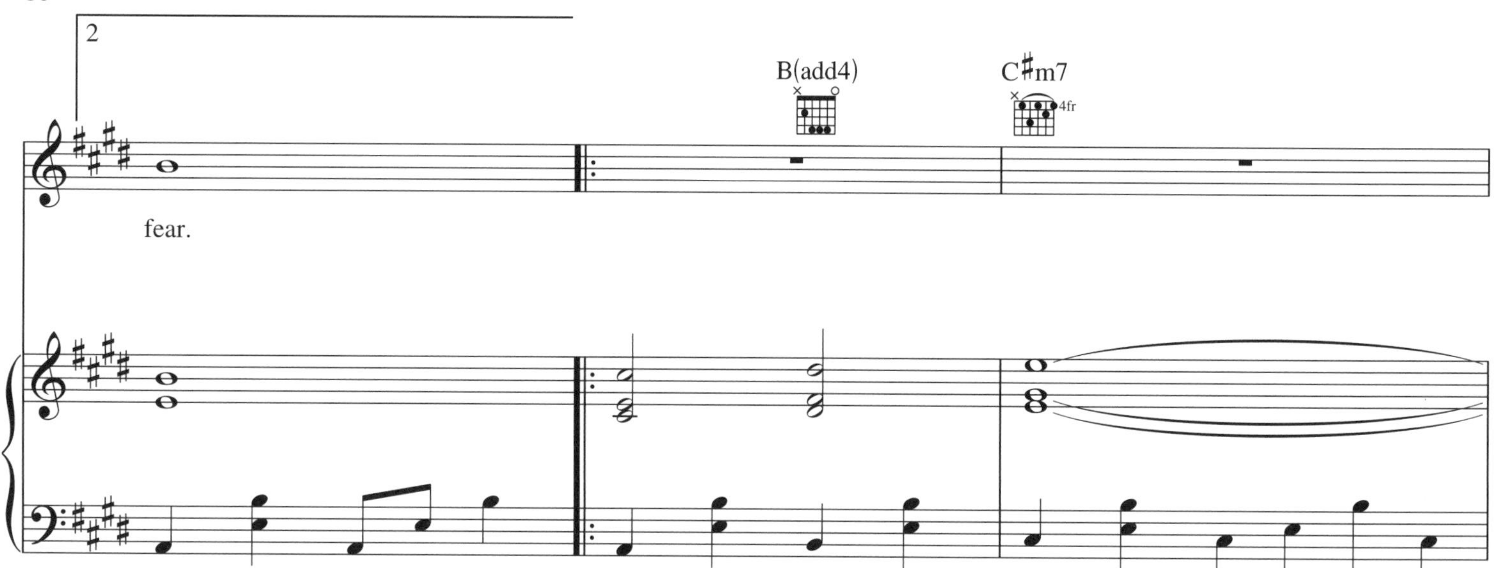
2
B(add4)
C♯m7
4fr
fear.

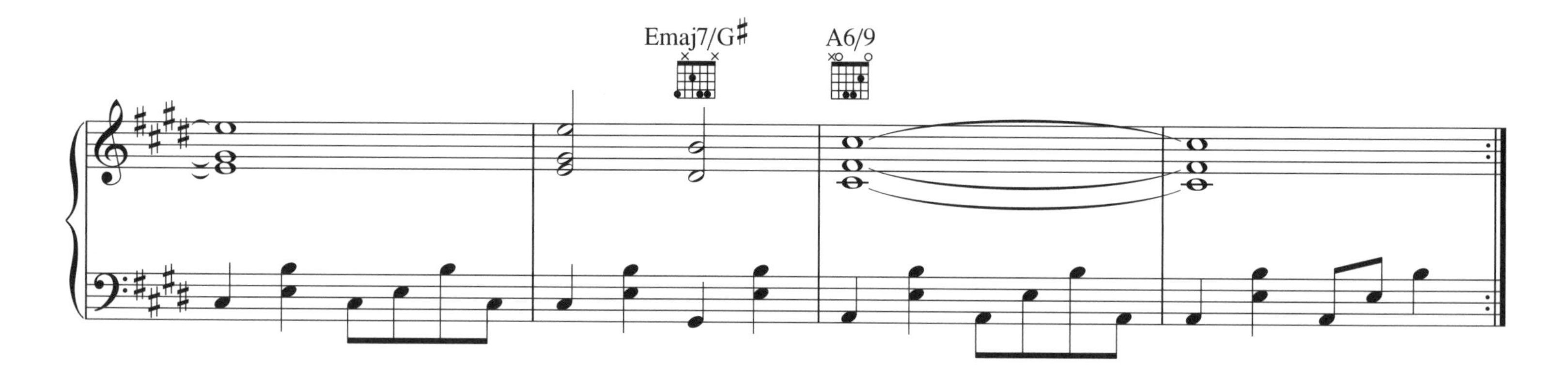
Emaj7/G♯
A6/9

A
Emaj7/G♯
E
E/G♯
I can't go wrong

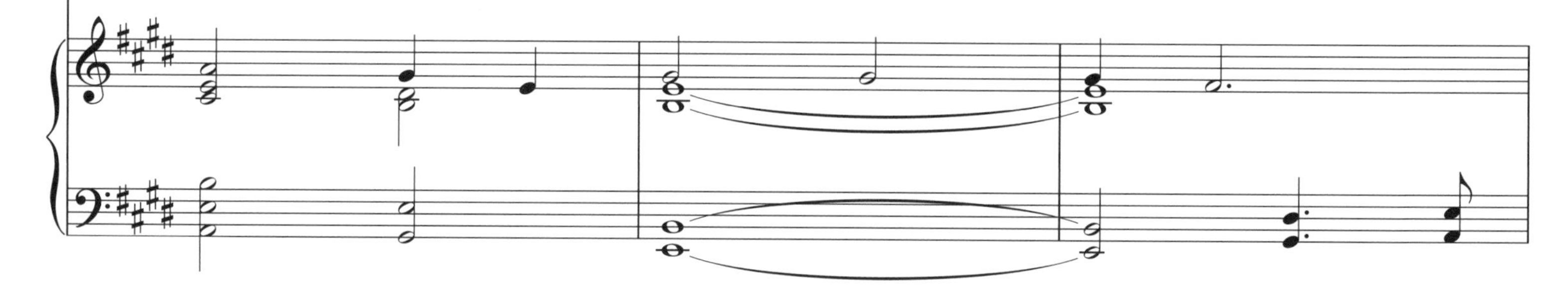

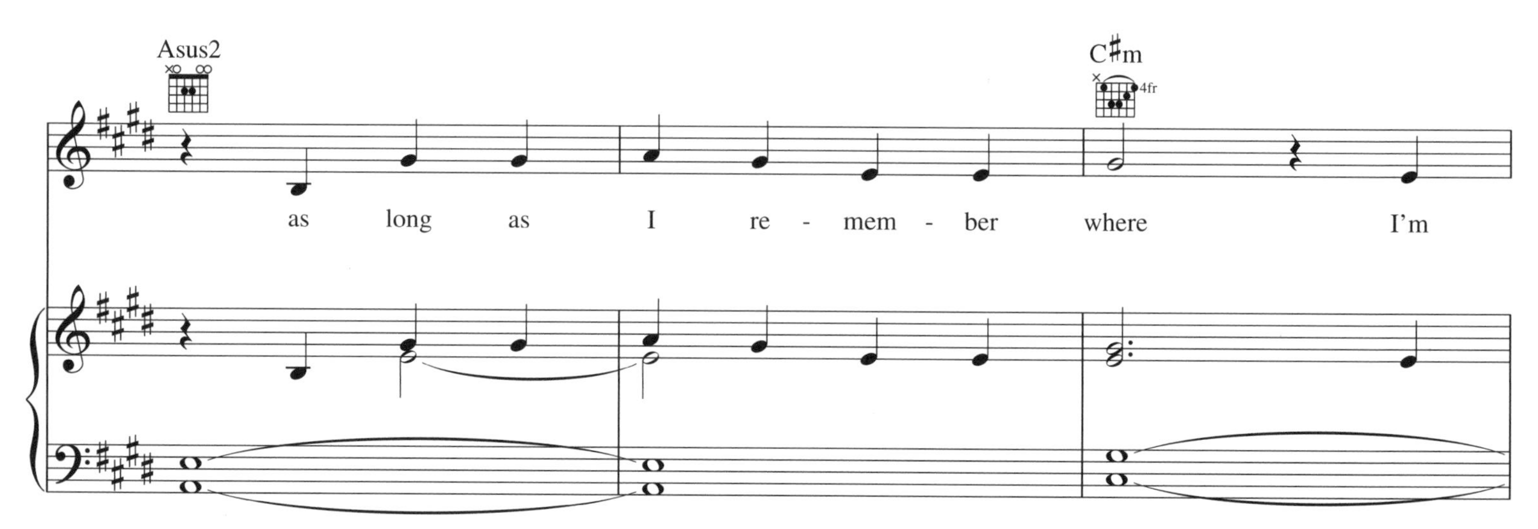
Asus2
C♯m
4fr
as long as I re - mem - ber where I'm

E/G♯
A5
5fr
from,
hold my head up just to
E5
E/G♯
A
keep it clear.
I want a chance to
C♯m
4fr
E/G♯
Asus2
face my fear, oh.
I
E
E/G♯
Asus2
can't go wrong
as long as I re - mem - ber

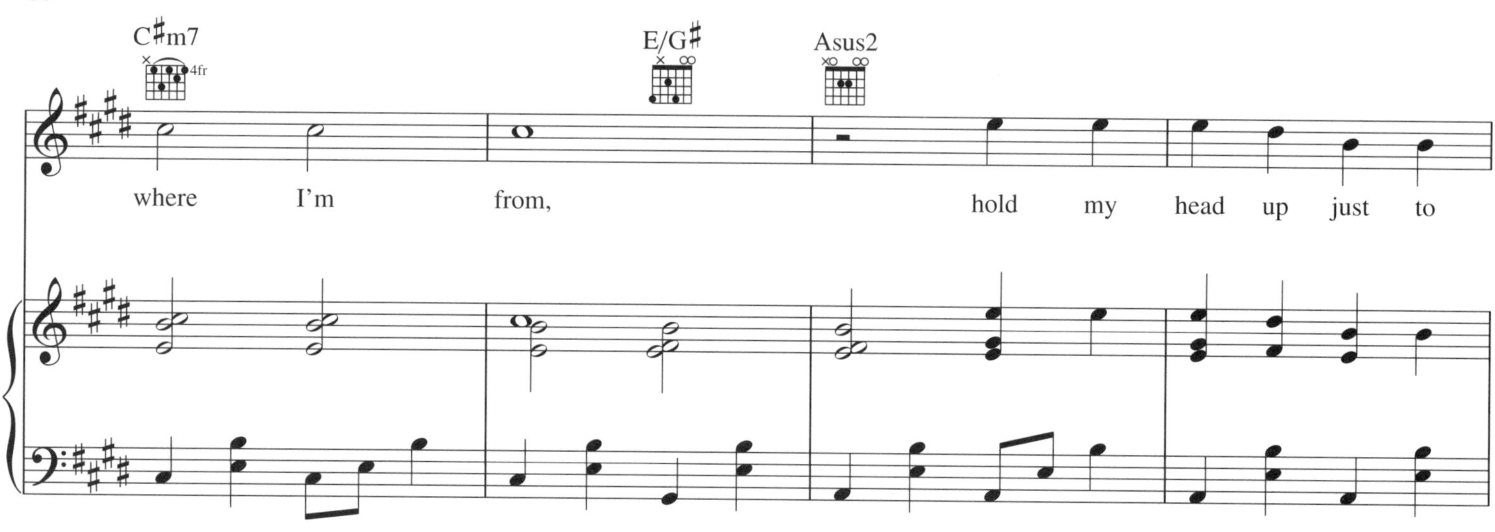
C♯m7
4fr
E/G♯
Asus2
where I'm from,
hold my head up just to

1
E
E/G♯
Asus2
keep it clear.
I want a

C♯m7
4fr
E/G♯
Asus2
chance _ just to face my fear,
face my

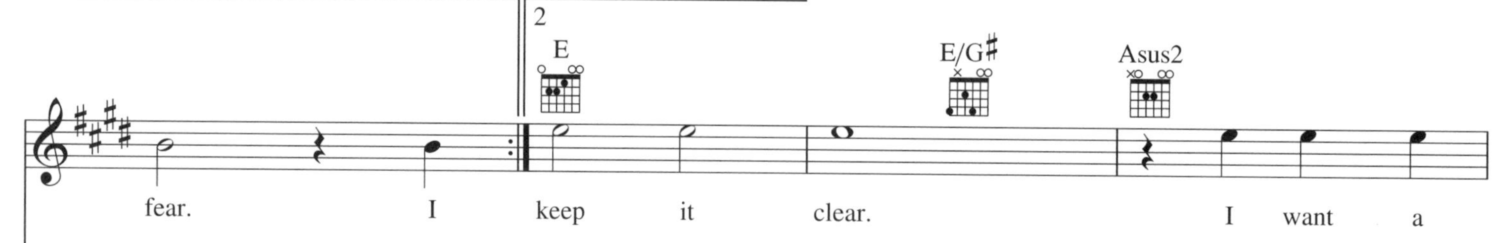
2
E
E/G♯
Asus2
fear.
I keep it clear.
I want a

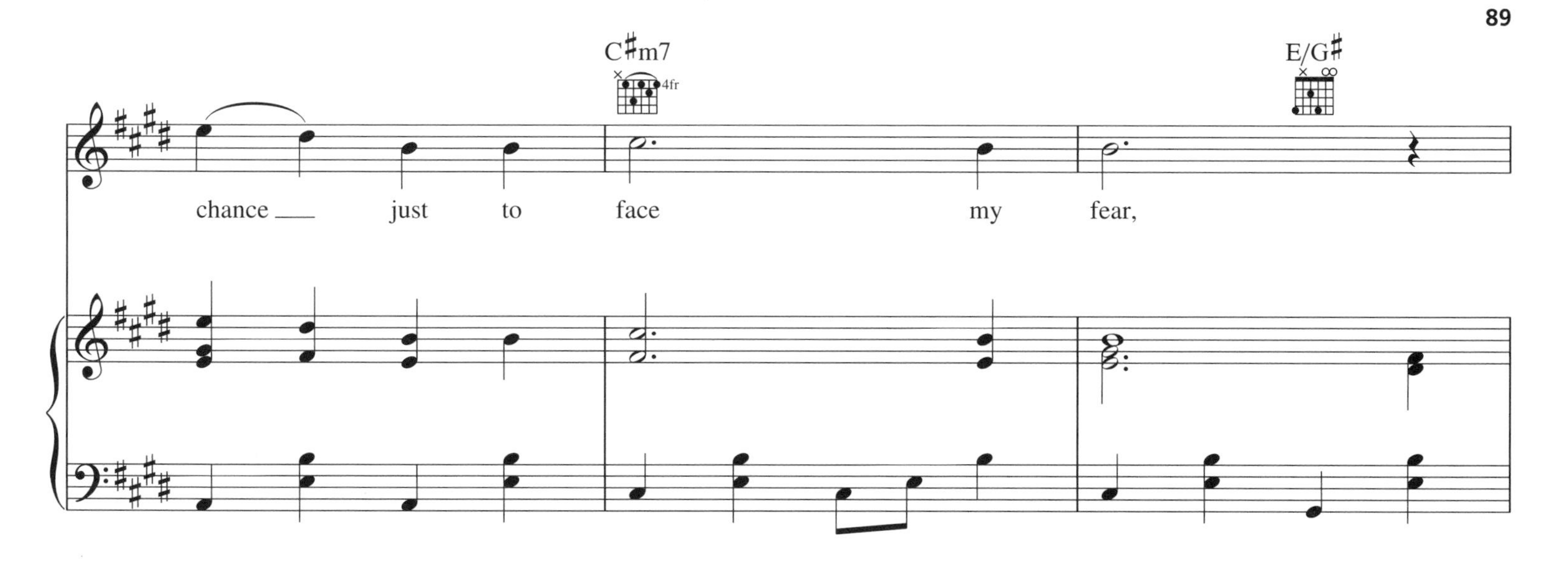
C♯m7
4fr
E/G♯
chance just to face my fear,

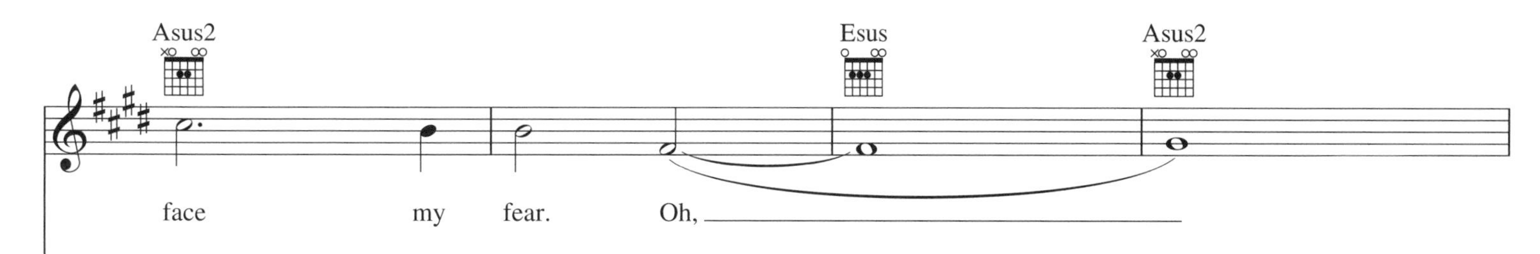
Asus2
Esus
Asus2
face my fear. Oh,

Asus2/G♯
F♯m7
Esus
just come a - long.

Asus2
Asus2/G♯
F♯m7
E5

A FOOL'S DANCE

Words and Music by
PHILLIP PHILLIPS

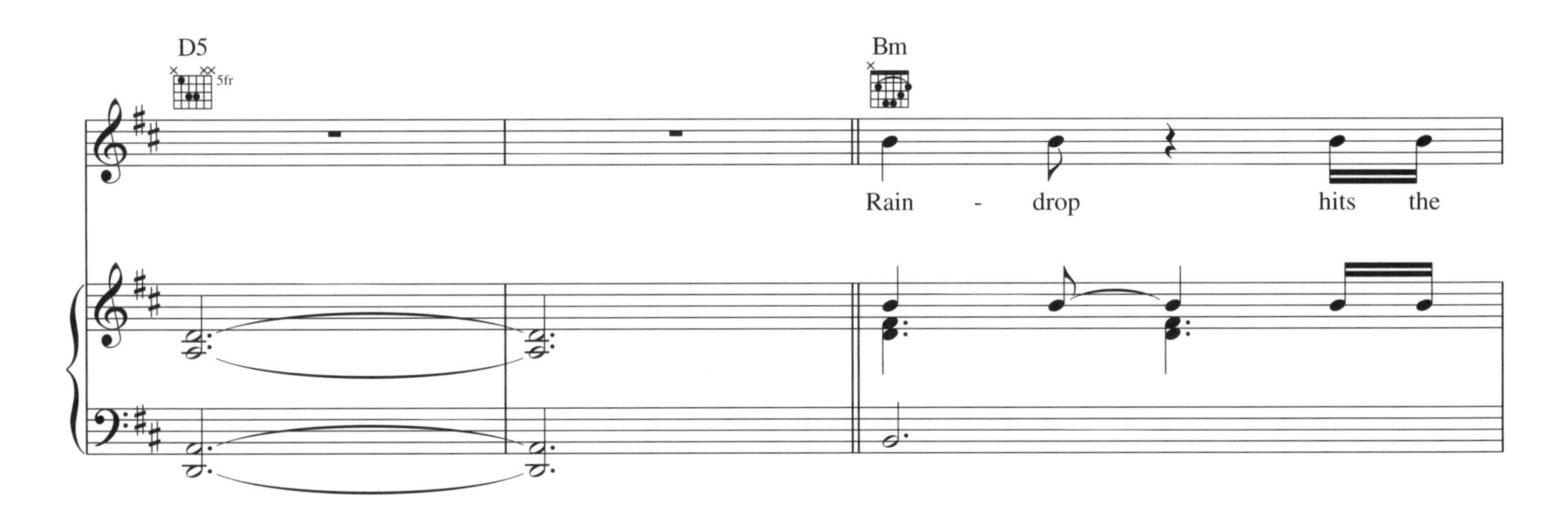

Bm
D5
5fr
porch to the cei - ling, makes it's way down to the floor.

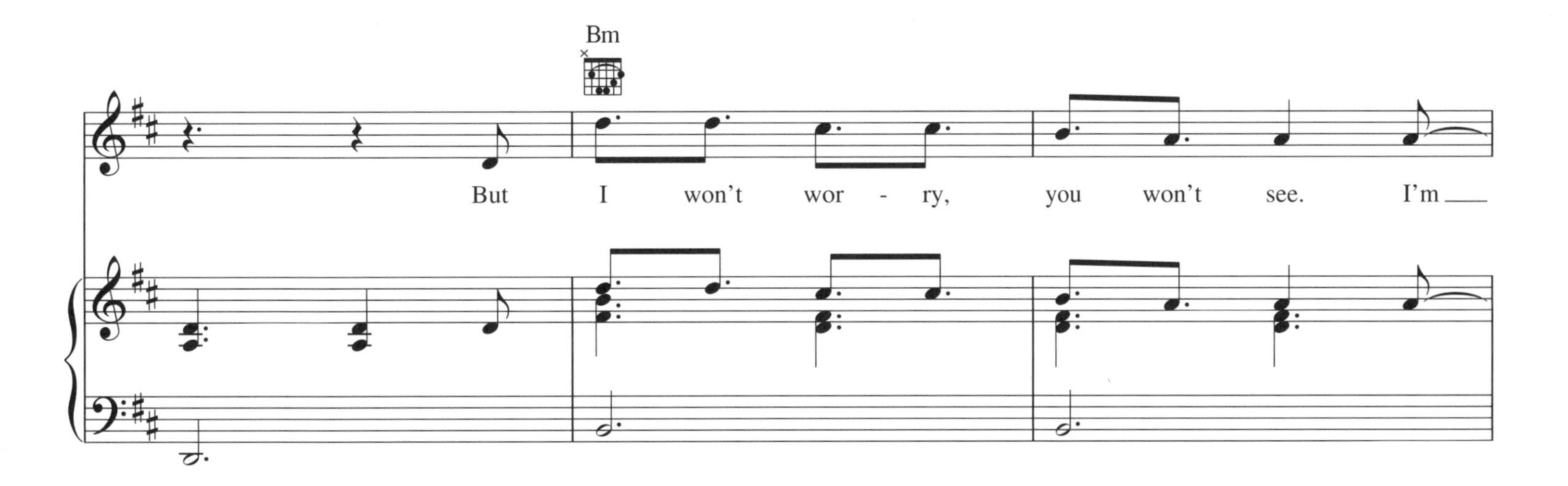
Bm
But I won't wor - ry, you won't see. I'm

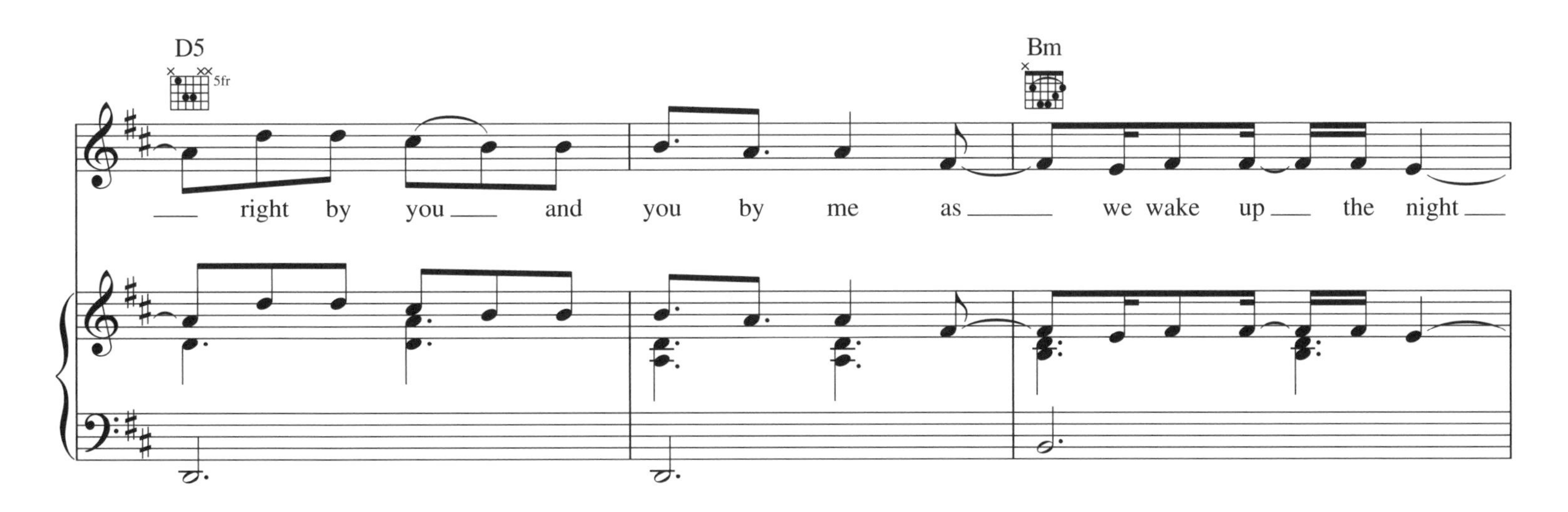
D5
5fr
Bm
right by you and you by me as we wake up the night

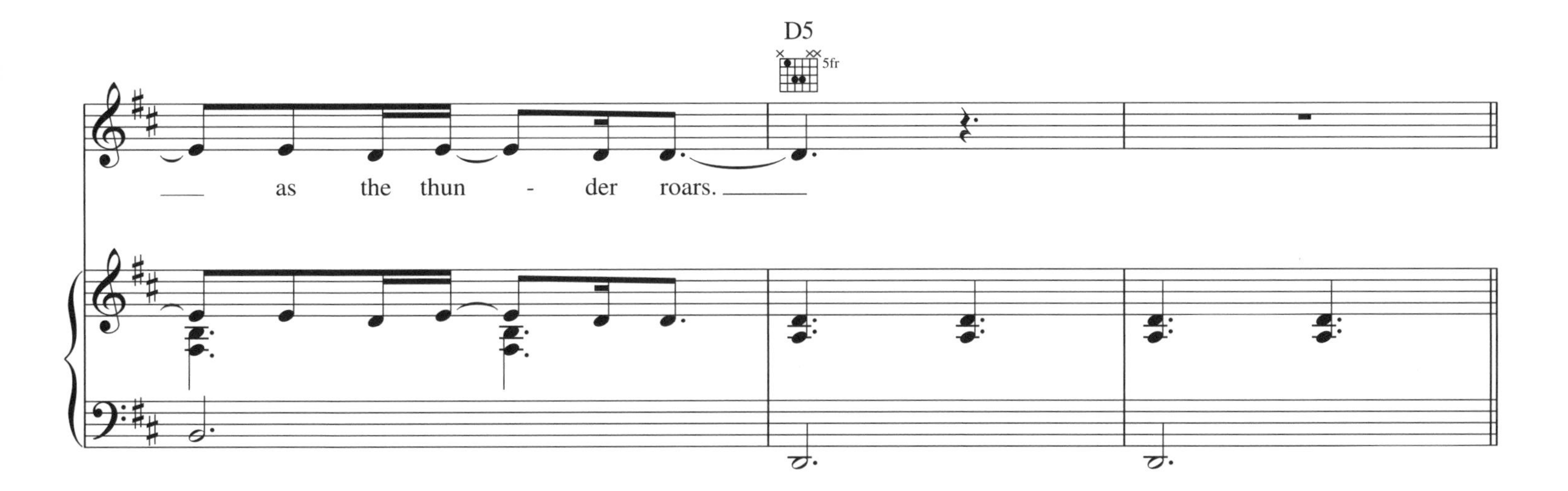
D5
5fr
as the thun - der roars.

G/B
D5
5fr

Bm
Stair - case could nev - er teach me more.

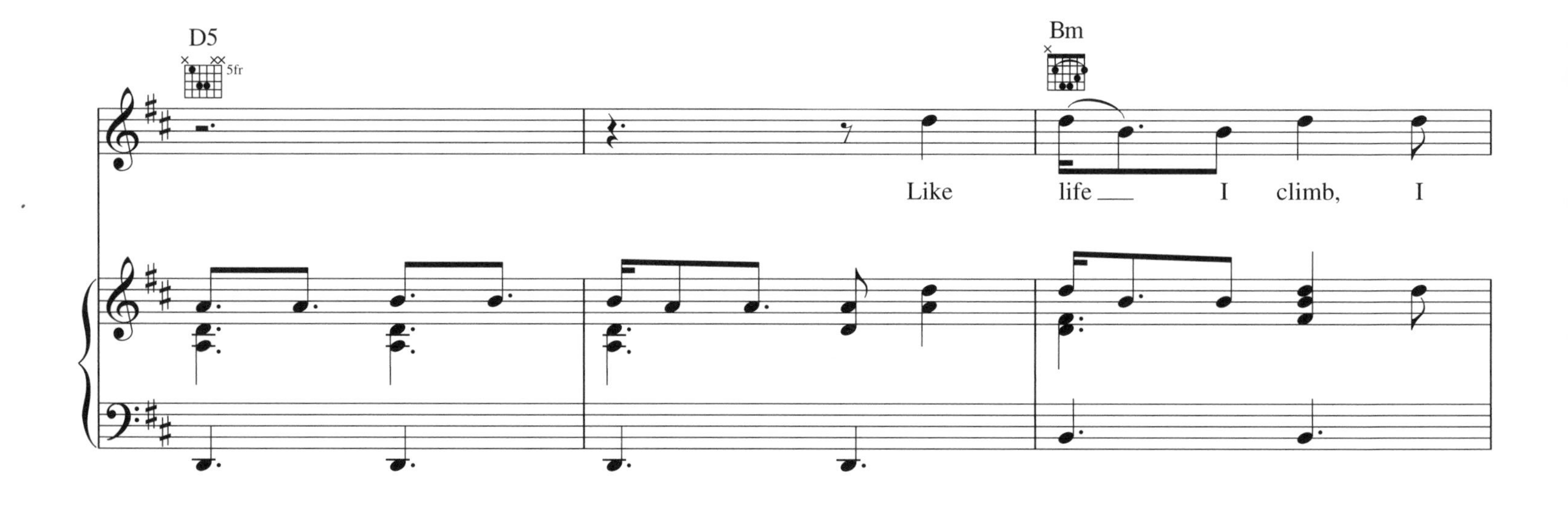
D5
5fr
Bm
Like life I climb, I

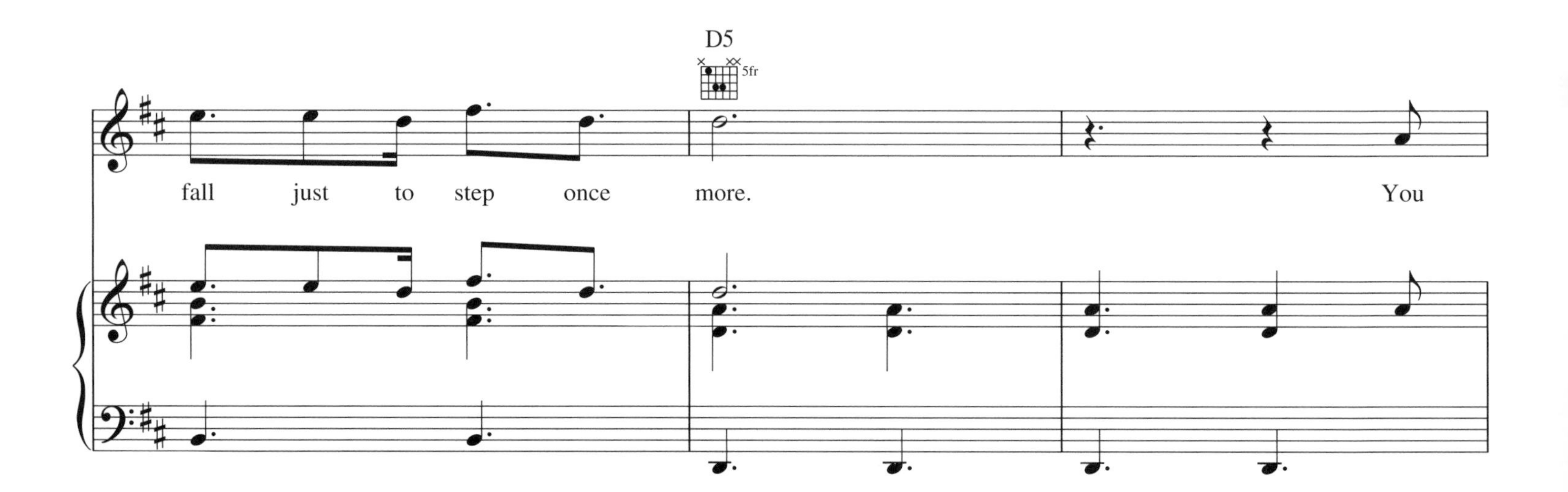
D5
5fr
fall just to step once more. You

Bm
D5
5fr
tricked me, fooled me, I was yours.

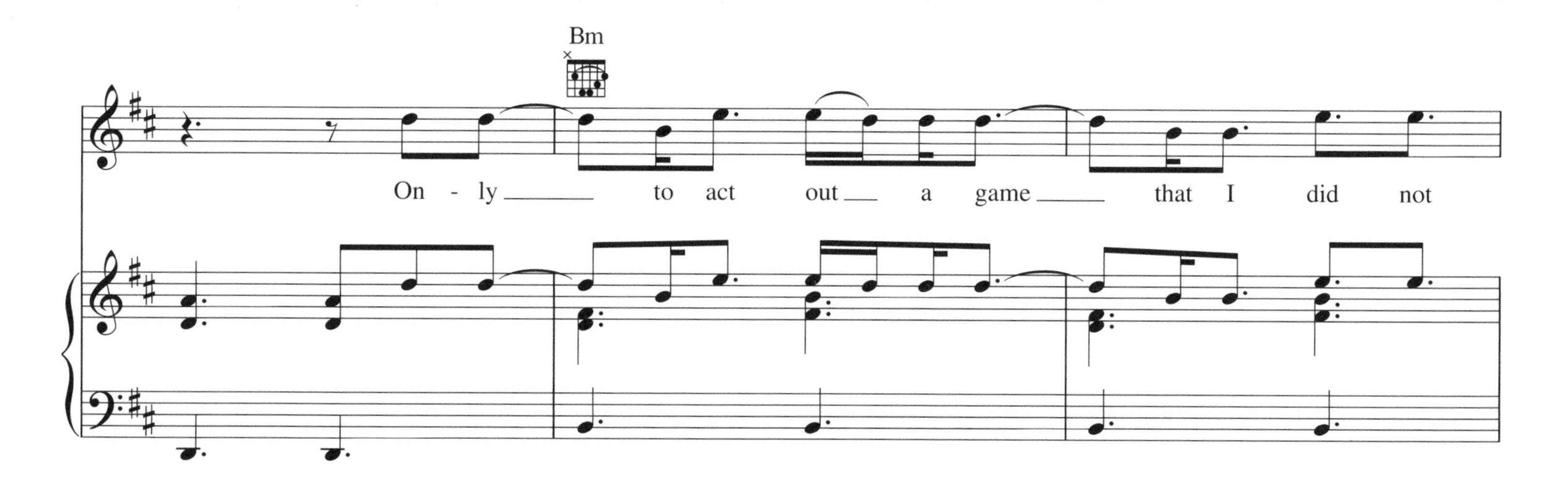
Bm
On - ly to act out a game that I did not

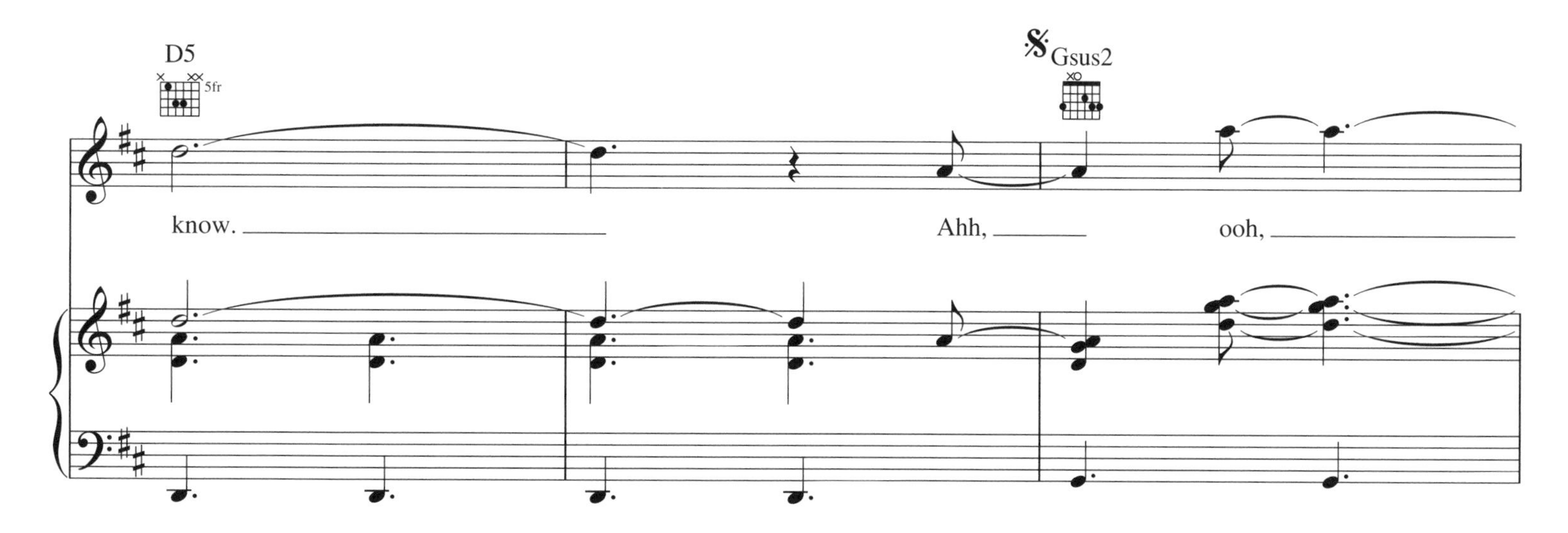
D5
5fr
Gsus2
know. Ahh, ooh,

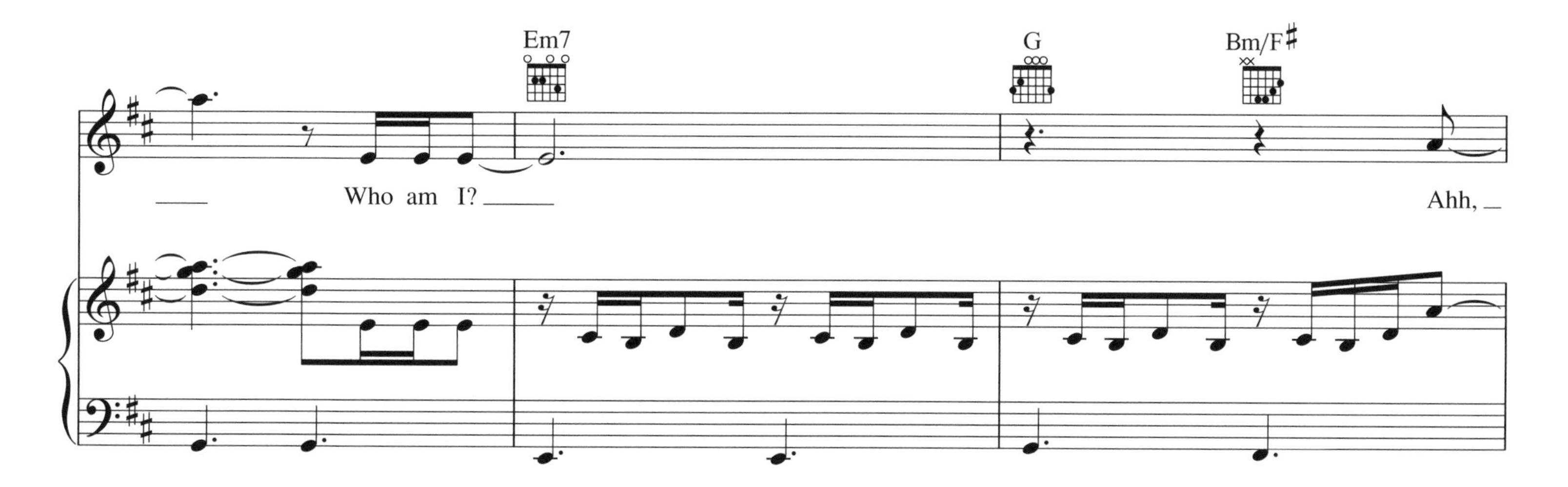
Em7
G
Bm/F♯
Who am I? Ahh,

Gsus2
Em7
ooh, Who am I an - y - more?

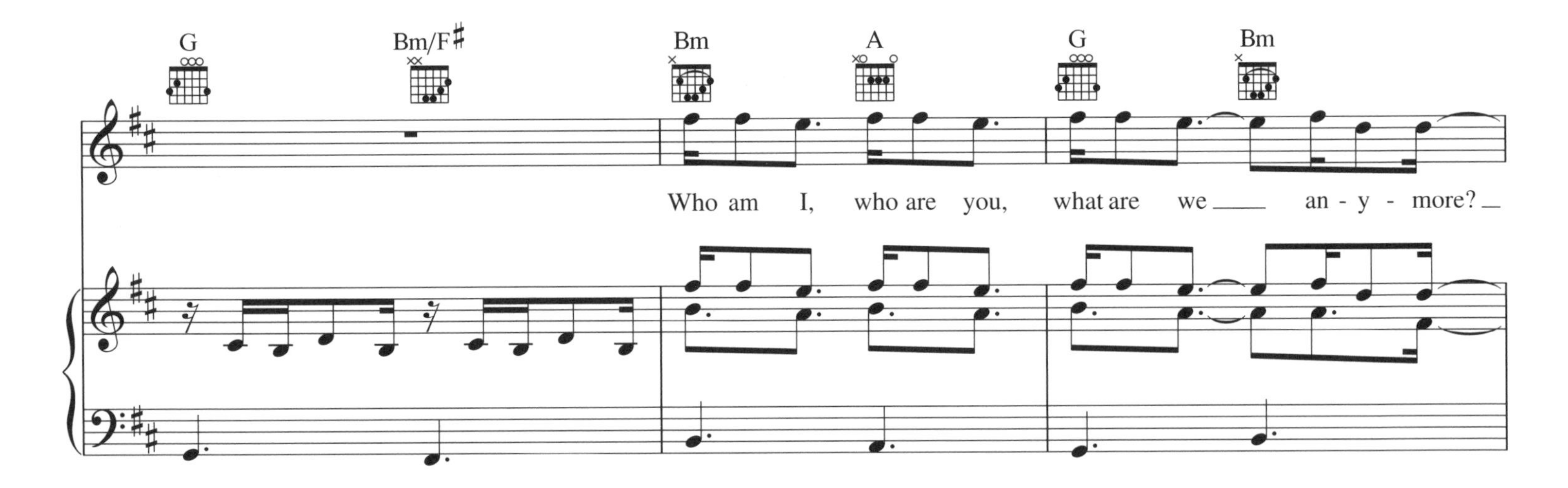
G
Bm/F♯
Bm
A
G
Bm
Who am I, who are you, what are we an - y - more?

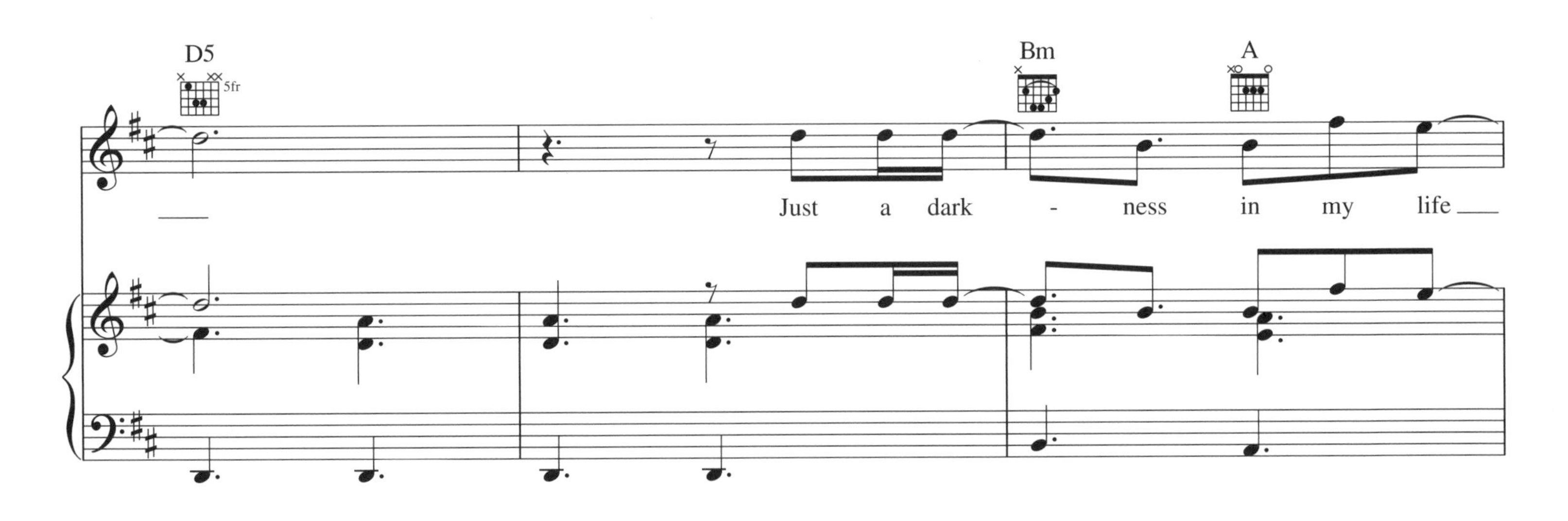
D5
5fr
Bm
A
Just a dark - ness in my life

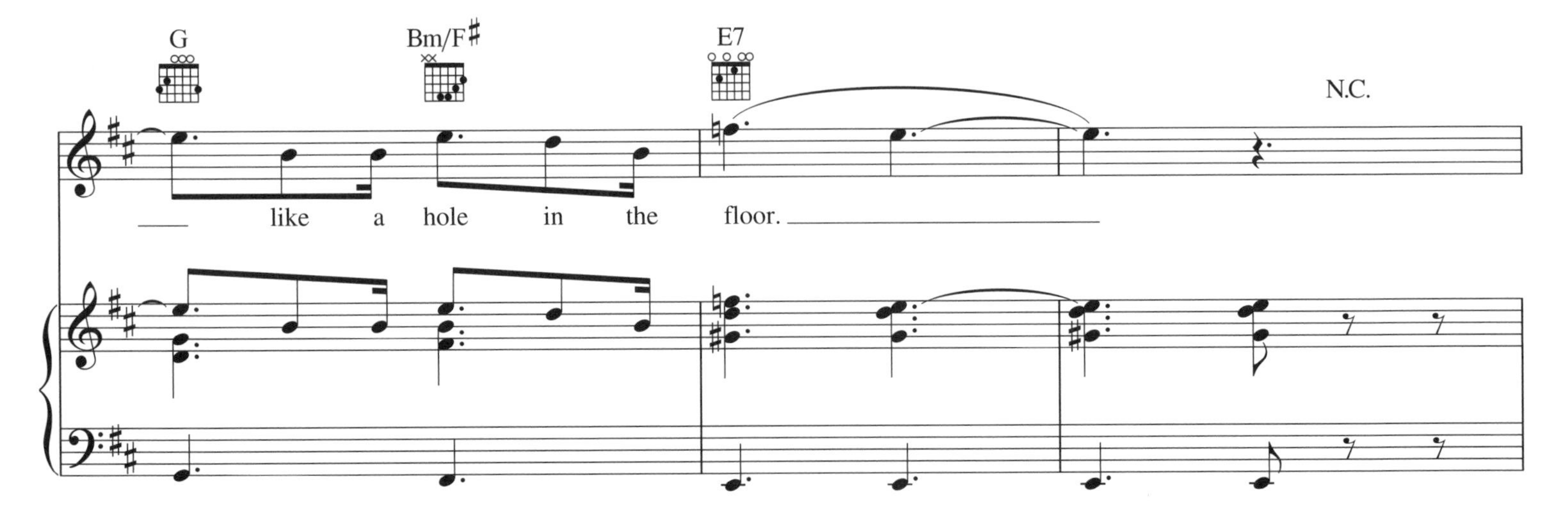
G
Bm/F♯
E7
N.C.
like a hole in the floor.

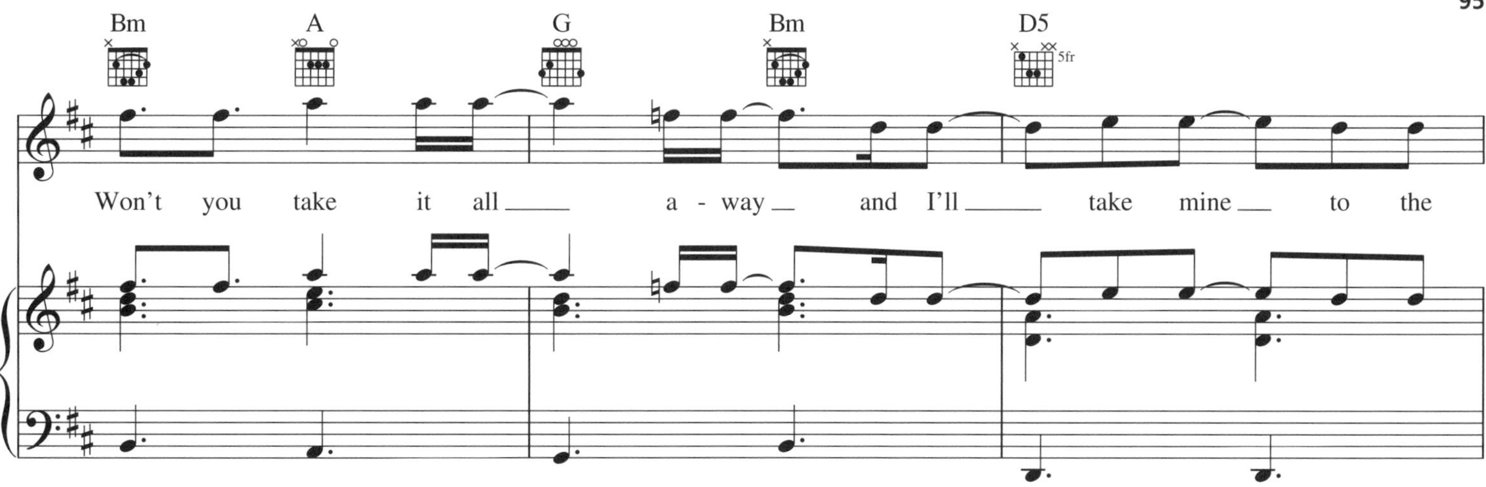
Bm
A
G
Bm
D5
5fr
Won't you take it all a - way and I'll take mine to the

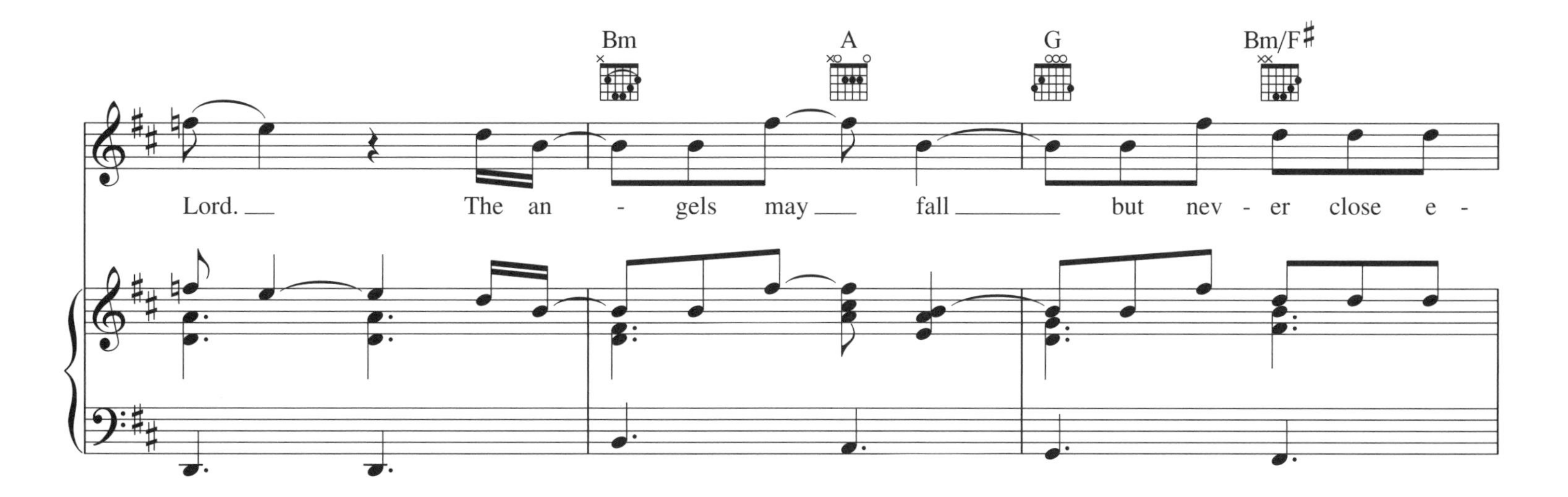
Bm
A
G
Bm/F♯
Lord. The an - gels may fall but nev - er close e -

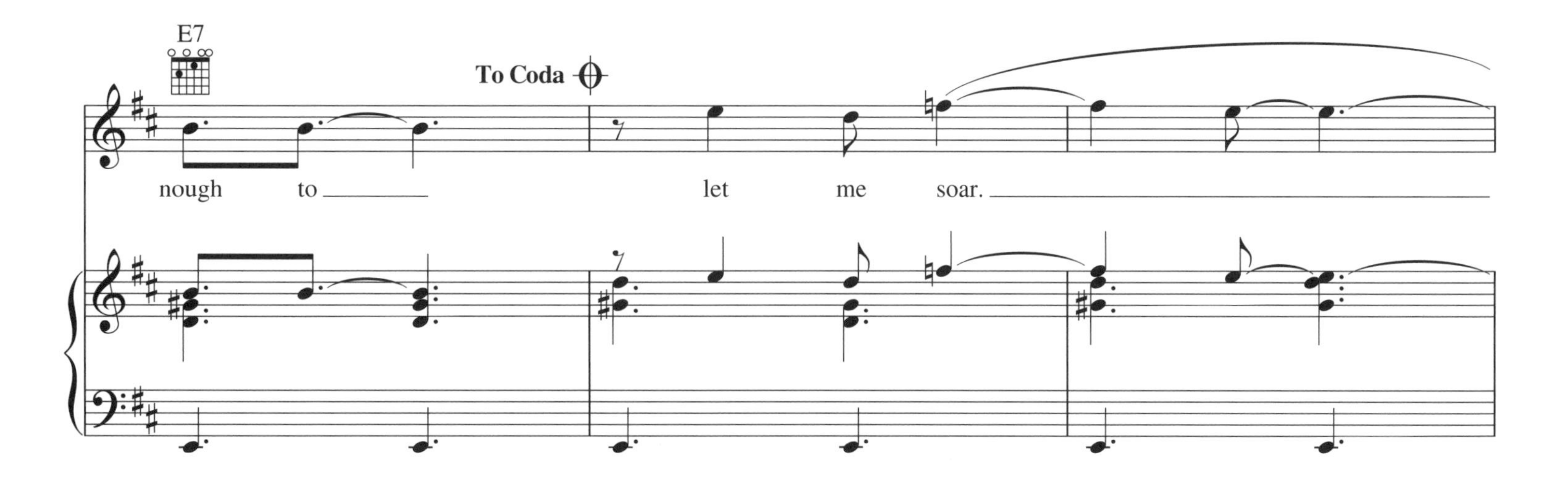
E7
To Coda
nough to let me soar.

Bm

D5
5fr
Bm

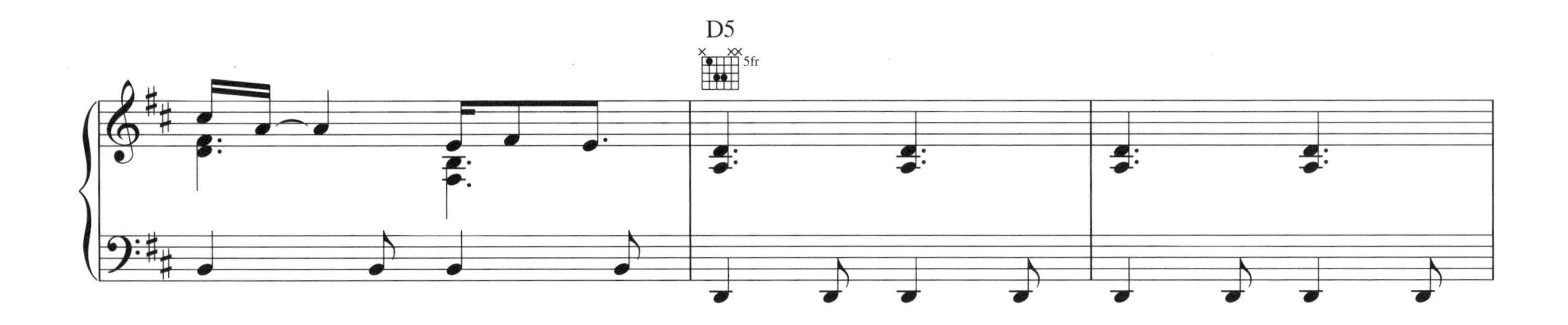
D5
5fr

Bm
D5
5fr
Eagles are flying and crows are dying, I guess I'll jump quick

Bm
just to see if I still have a chance to live.

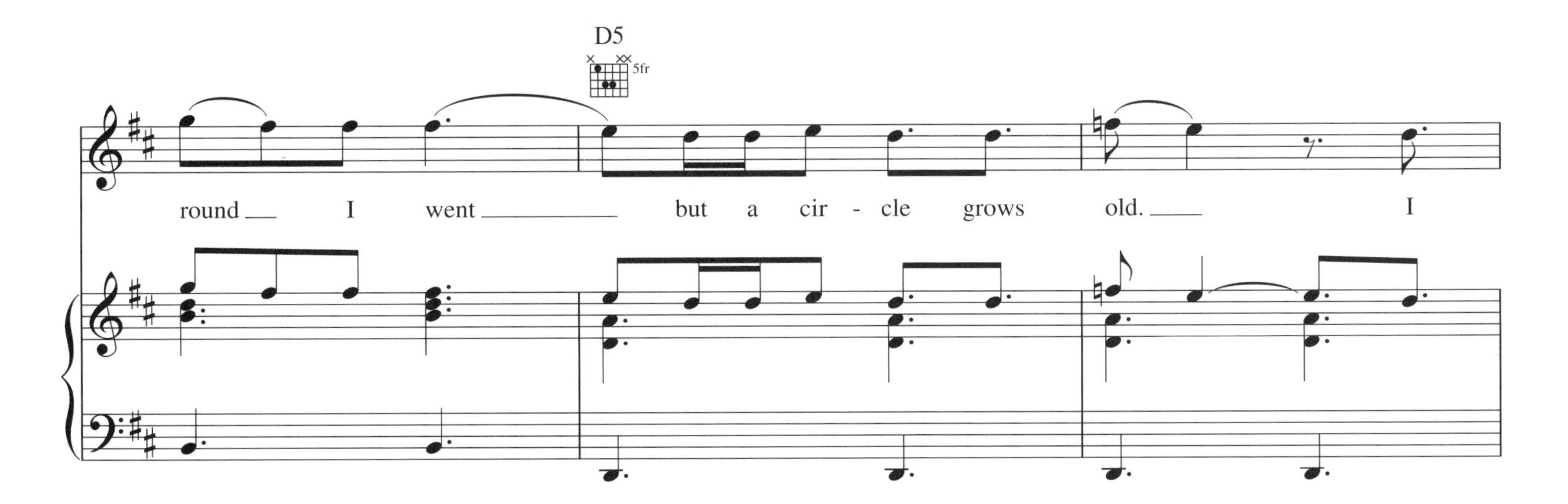

D.S. al Coda

home. Ahh,

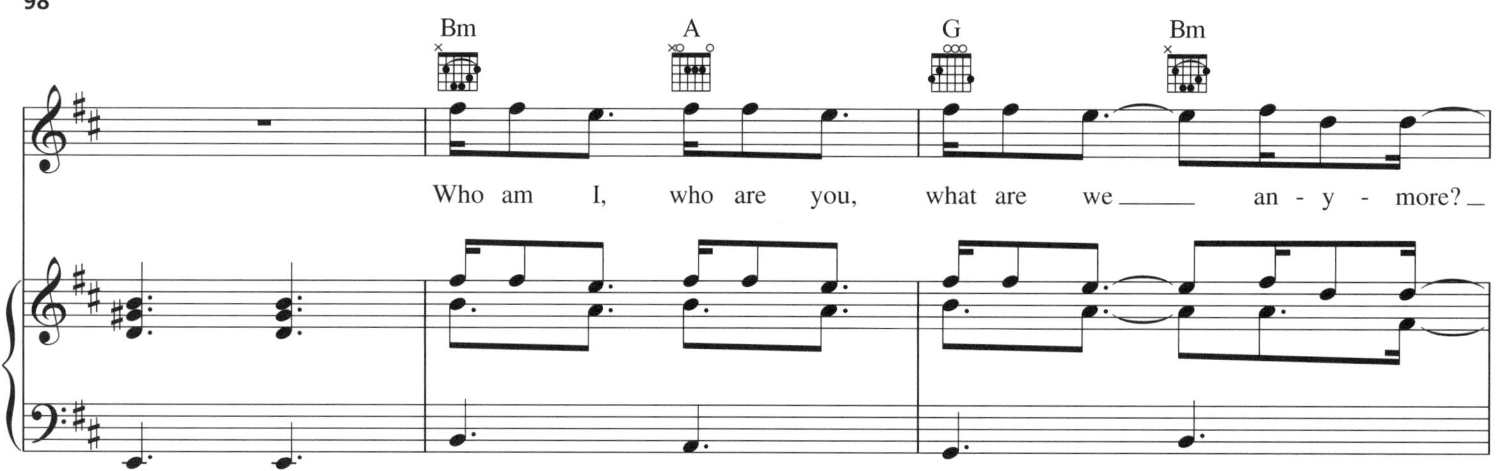
Bm
A
G
Bm
Who am I, who are you, what are we an - y - more?

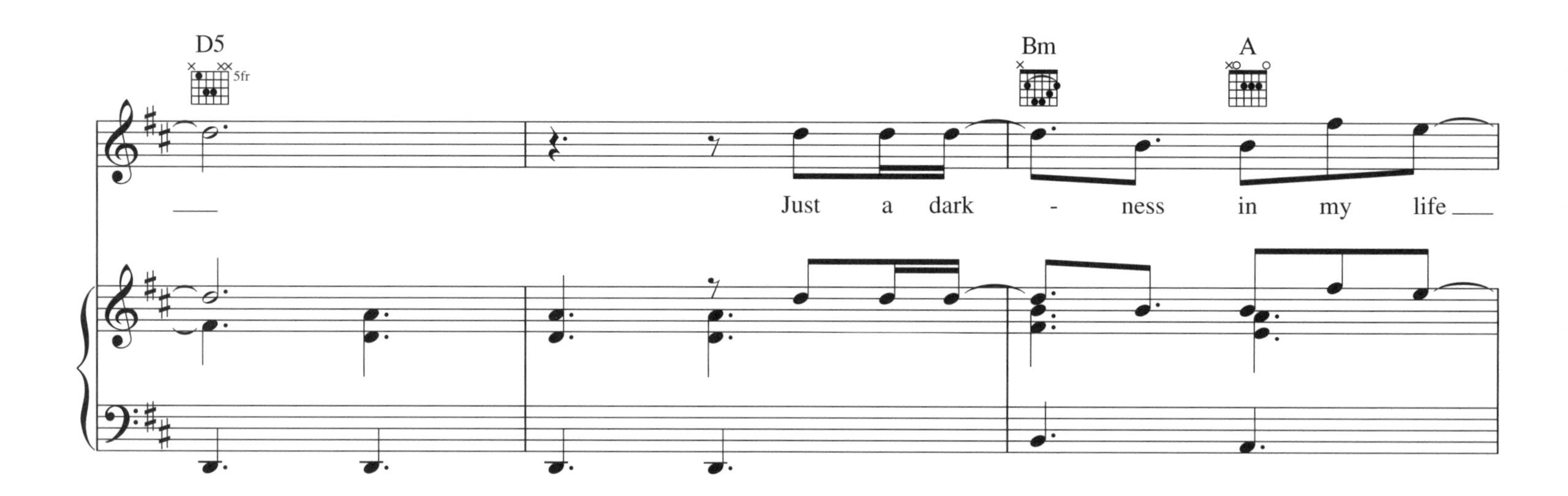
D5
5fr
Bm
A
Just a dark - ness in my life

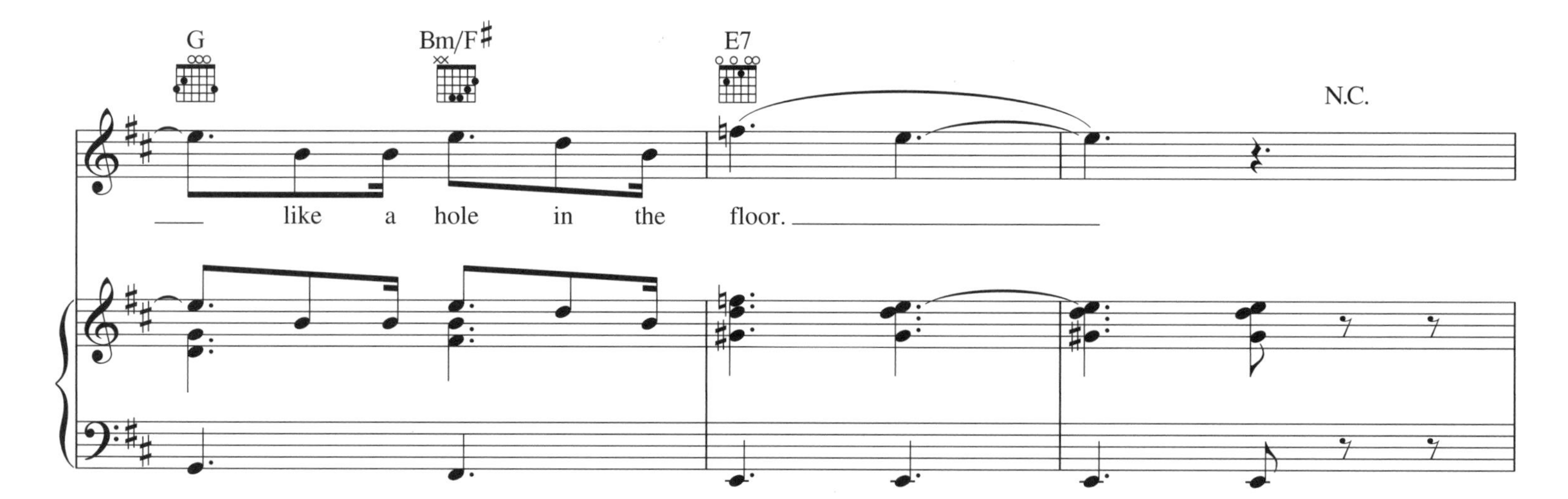
G
Bm/F♯
E7
N.C.
like a hole in the floor.

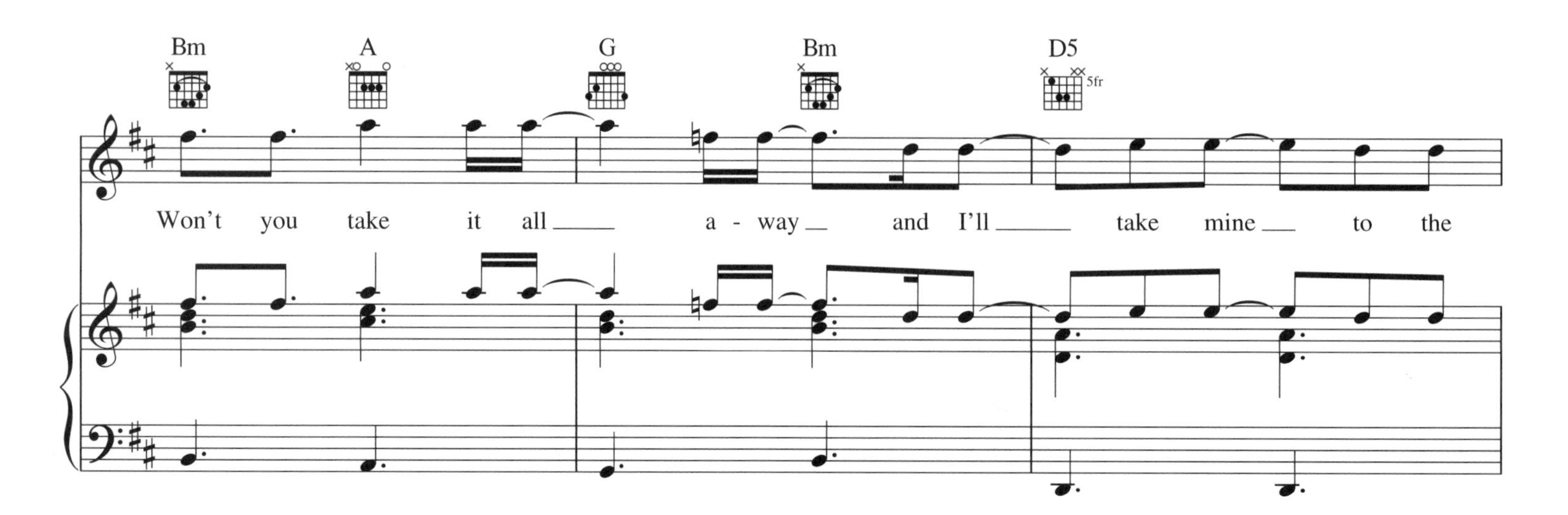
Bm
A
G
Bm
D5
5fr
Won't you take it all a - way and I'll take mine to the

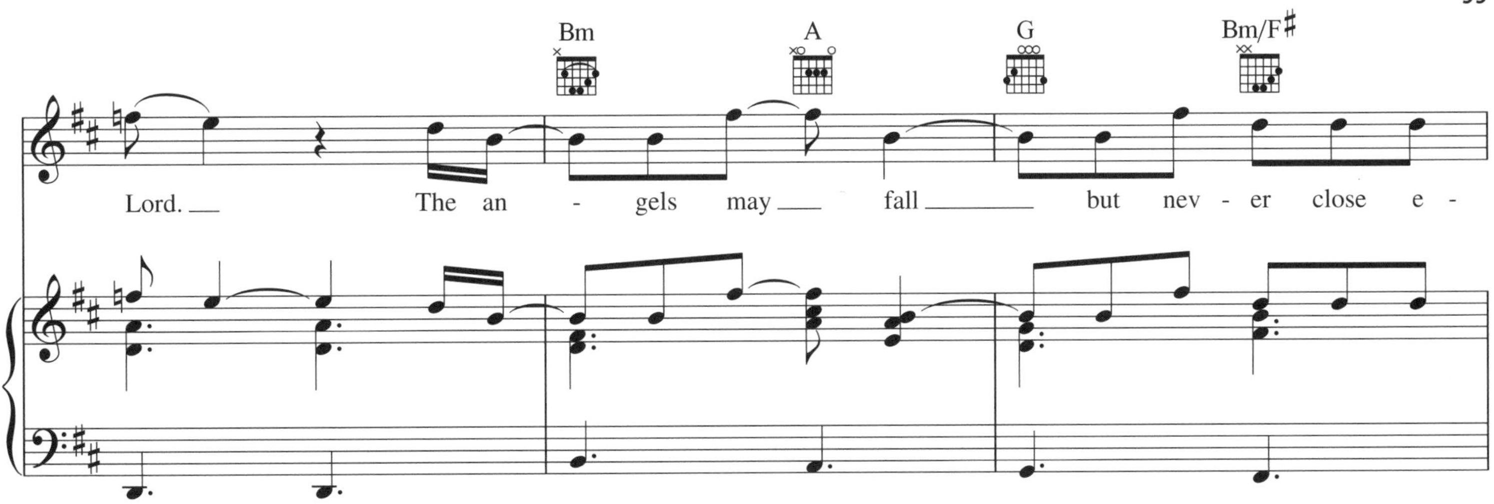
Bm
A
G
Bm/F♯
Lord. The an - gels may fall but nev - er close e -

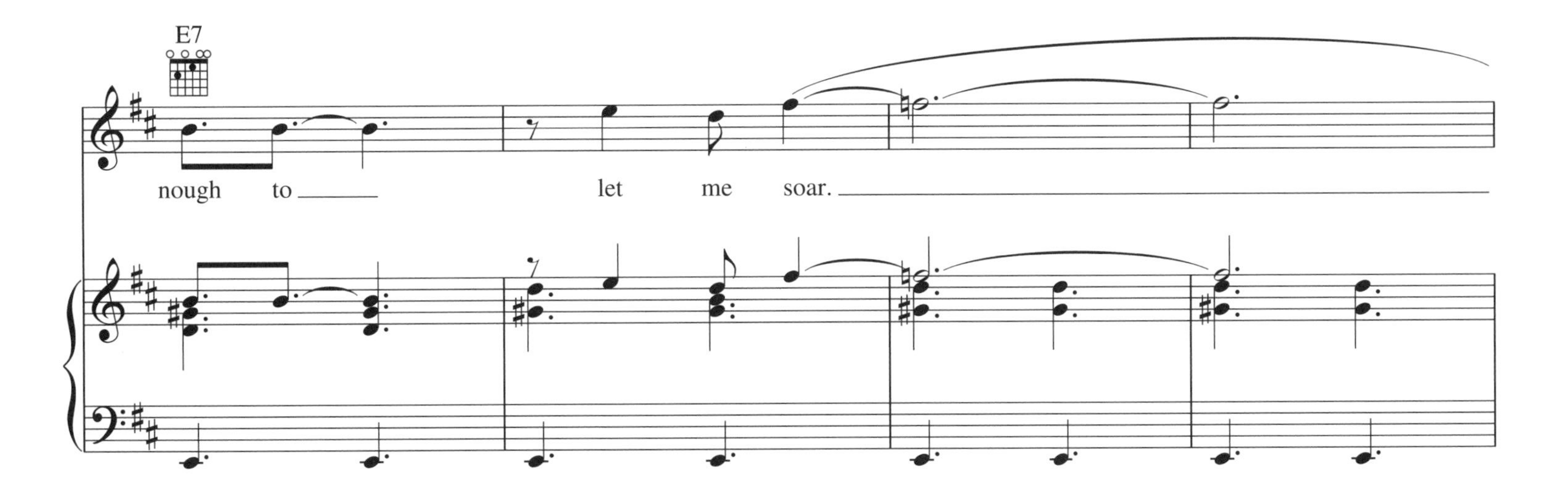
E7
nough to let me soar.

Bm
D5
5fr

Bm
D5
5fr

SO EASY

Words and Music by PETER AMATO,
PETER SALLIS and STEPHEN WRABEL

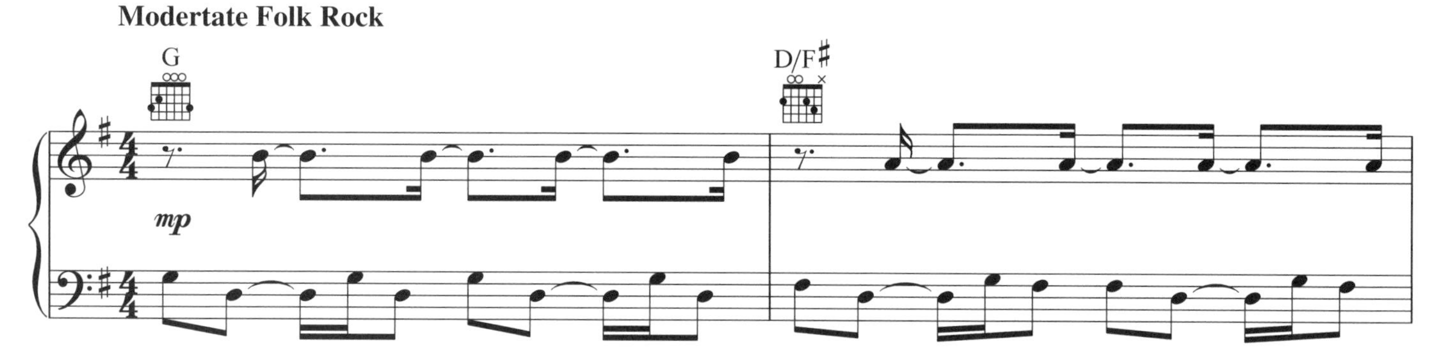

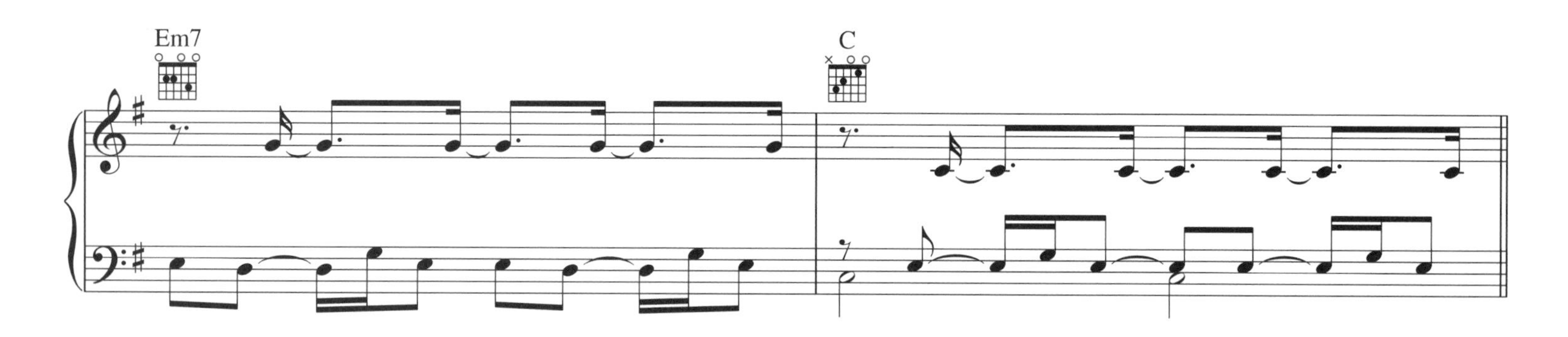

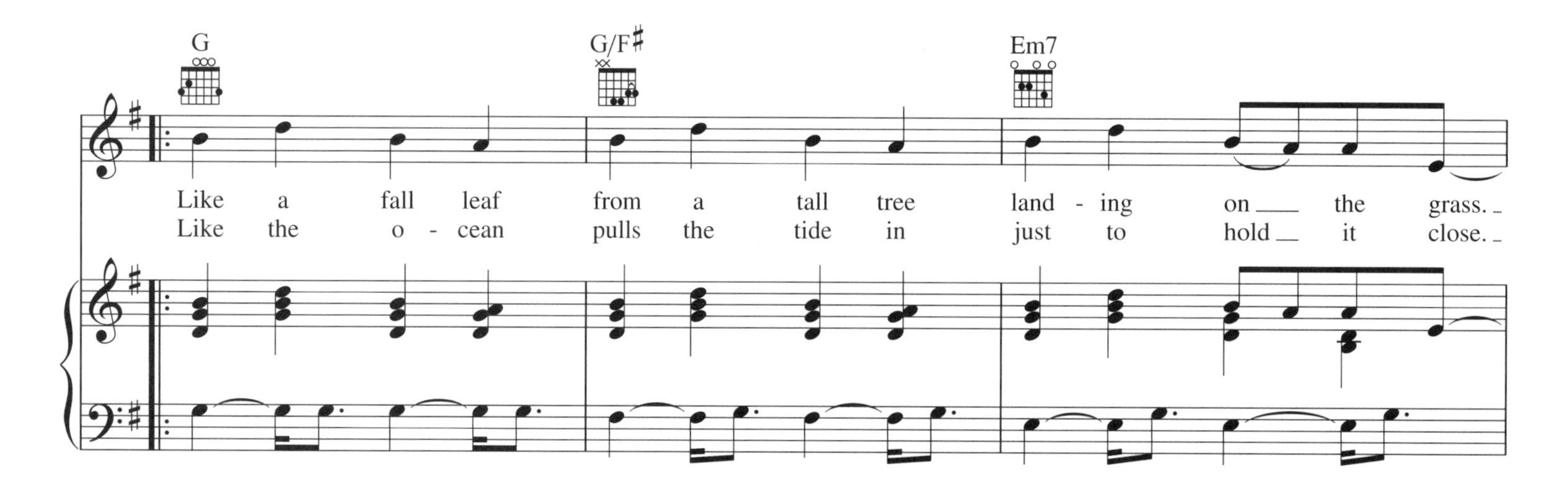

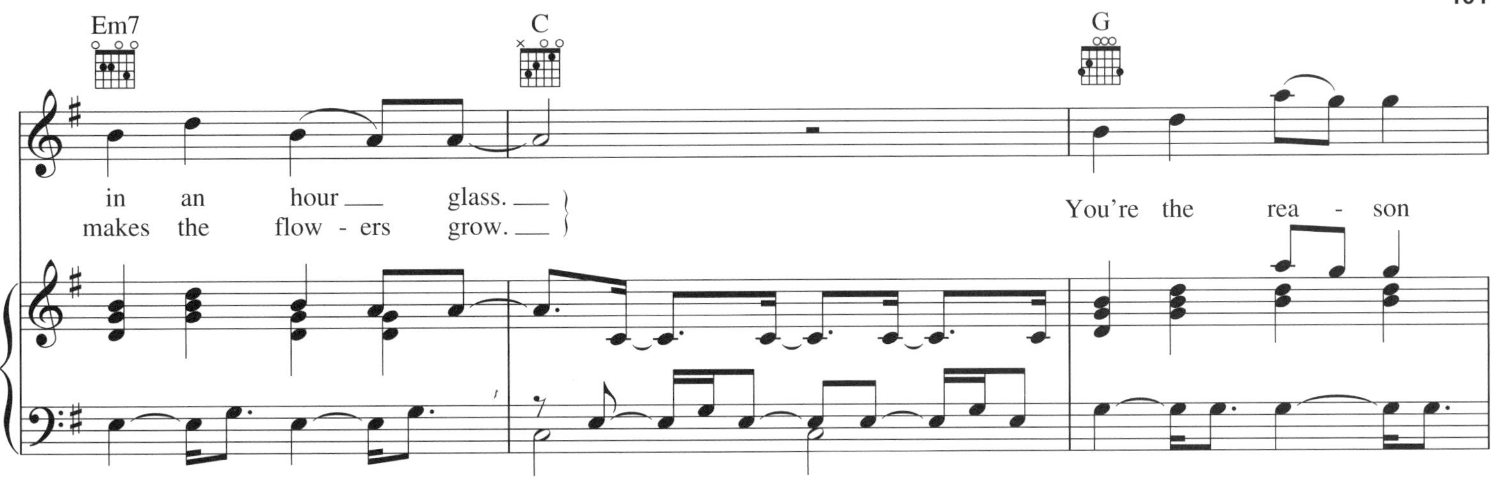
Em7
C
G
in an hour glass.
makes the flow - ers grow.
You're the rea - son

D5
Em
C
I be - lieve in some - thing I don't know.

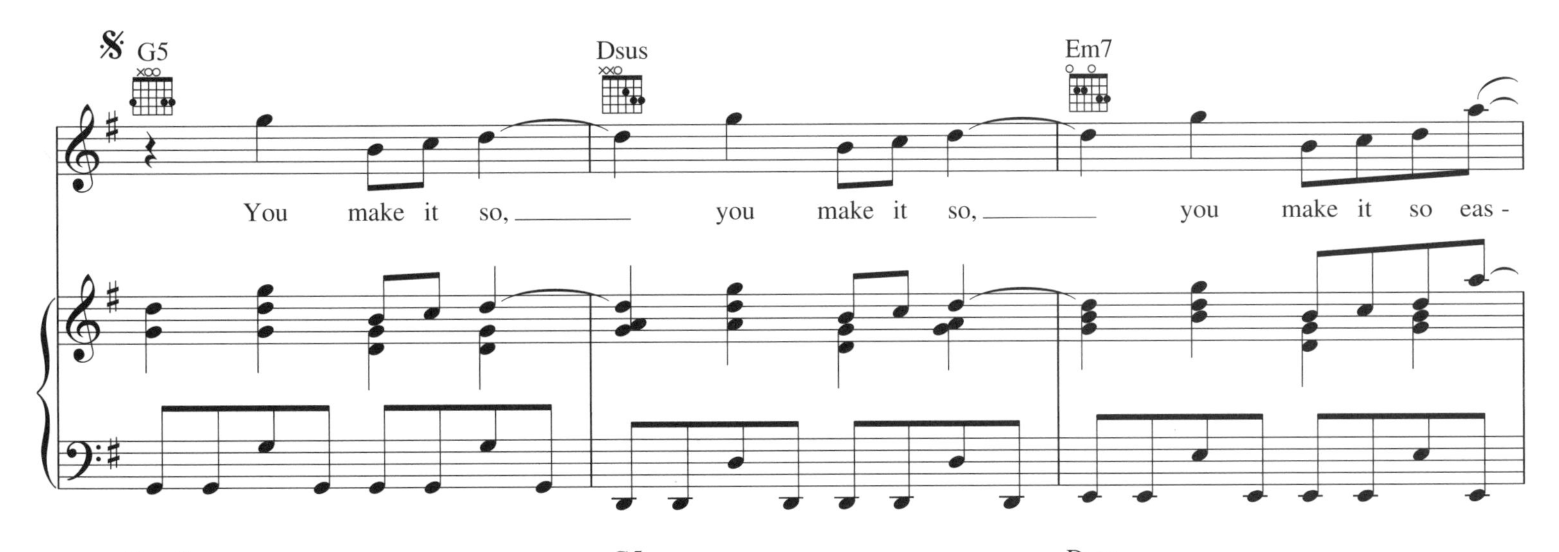
G5
Dsus
Em7
You make it so, you make it so, you make it so eas -

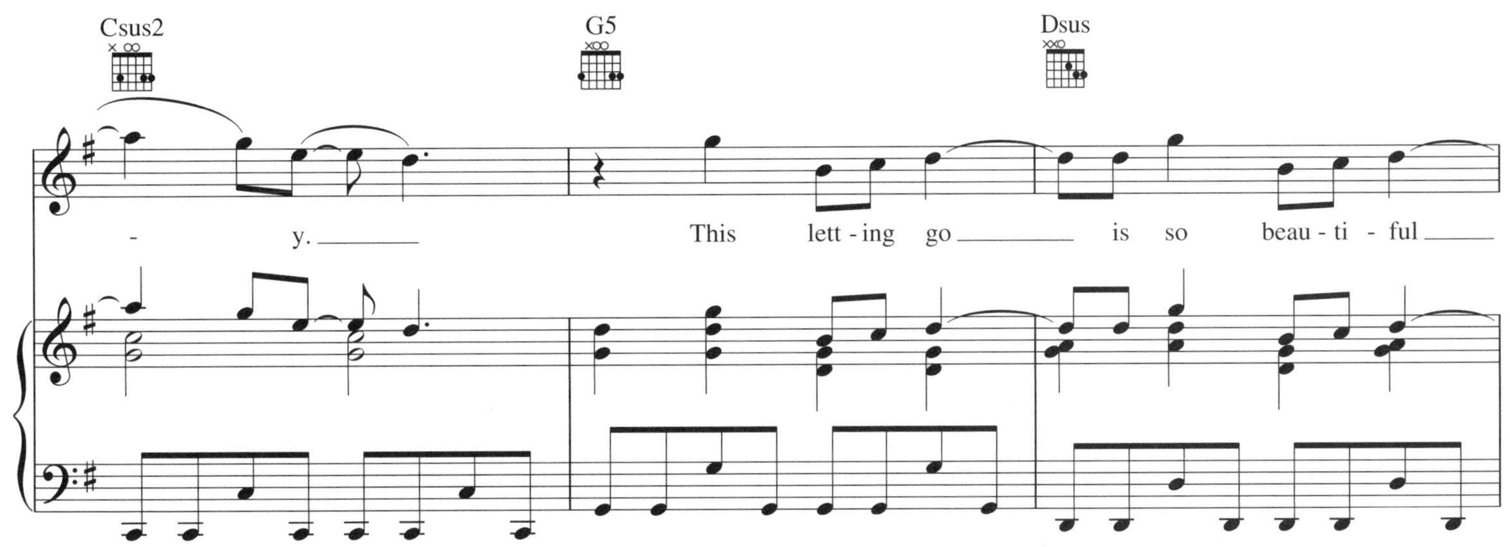
Csus2
G5
Dsus
- y. This lett - ing go is so beau - ti - ful

Em7
Csus2
To Coda
1 G
'cause you make it so eas - y to fall so hard.
G/F#
Em7
To fall so hard.
C
2
G5
Oh,

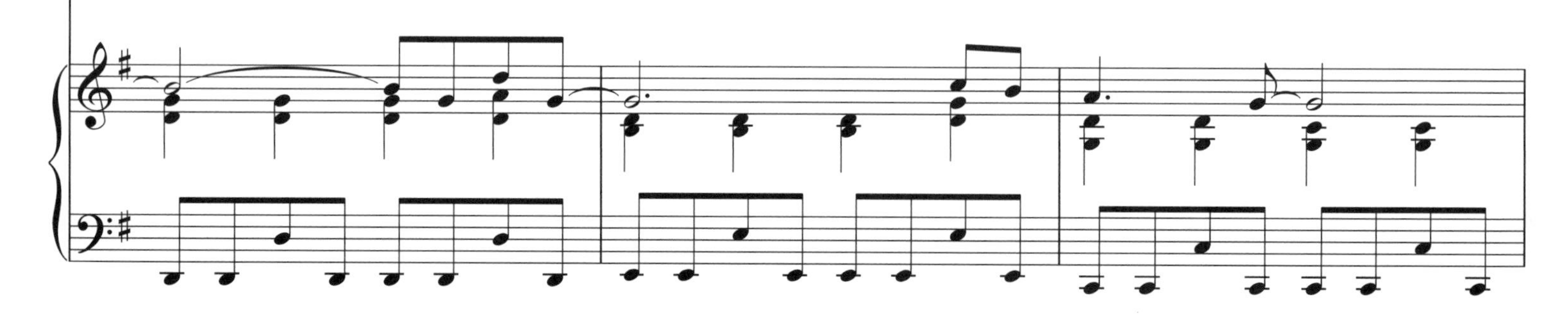
Dsus
Em7
Csus2
oh,
oh.

G5
Dsus
Em7
Oh, oh, oh.
Csus2
G5
D5
You make it so, you make it so,

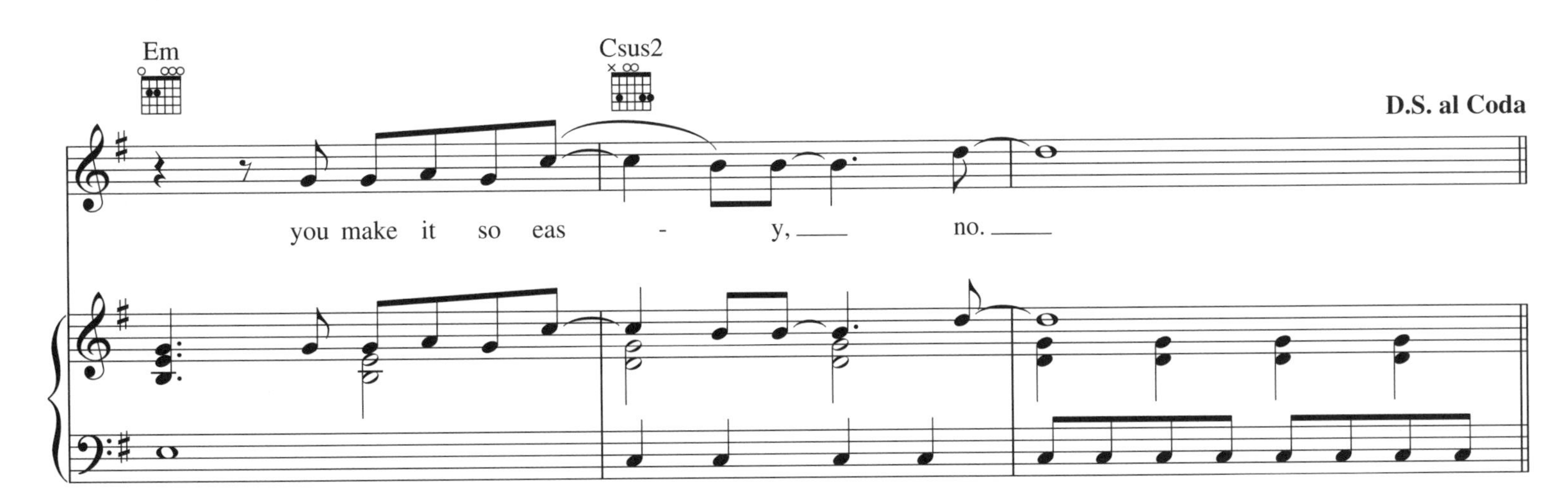
Em
Csus2
D.S. al Coda
you make it so eas - y, no.

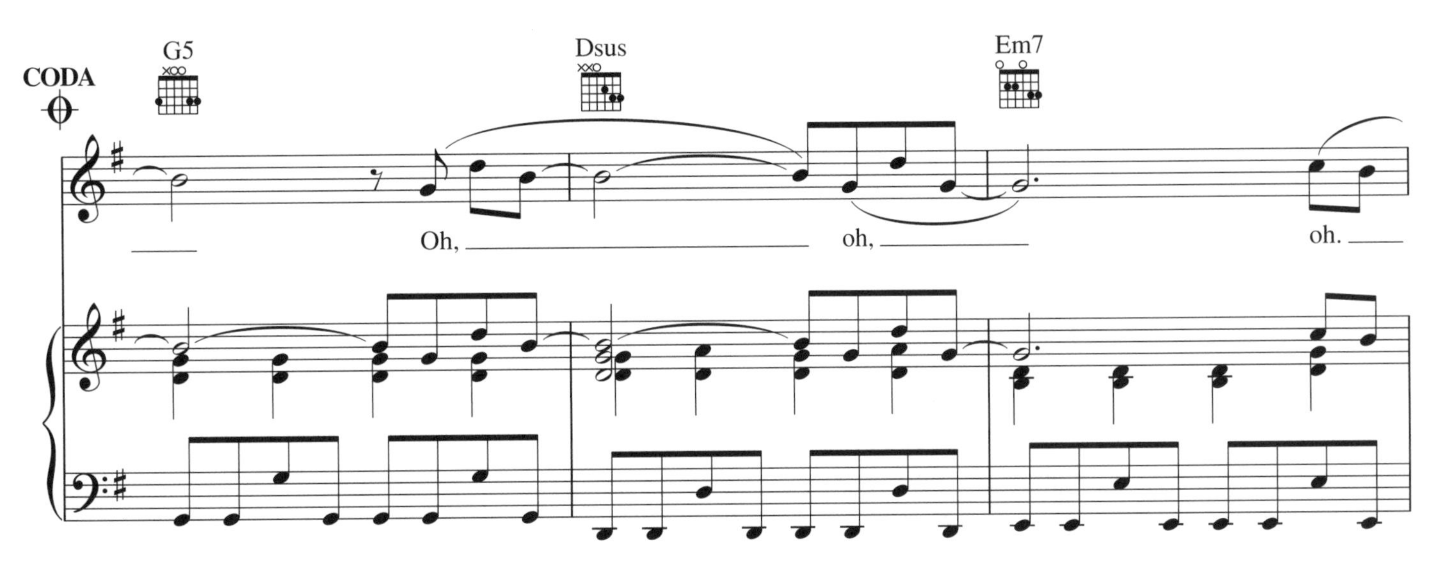
CODA
G5
Dsus
Em7
Oh, oh, oh.

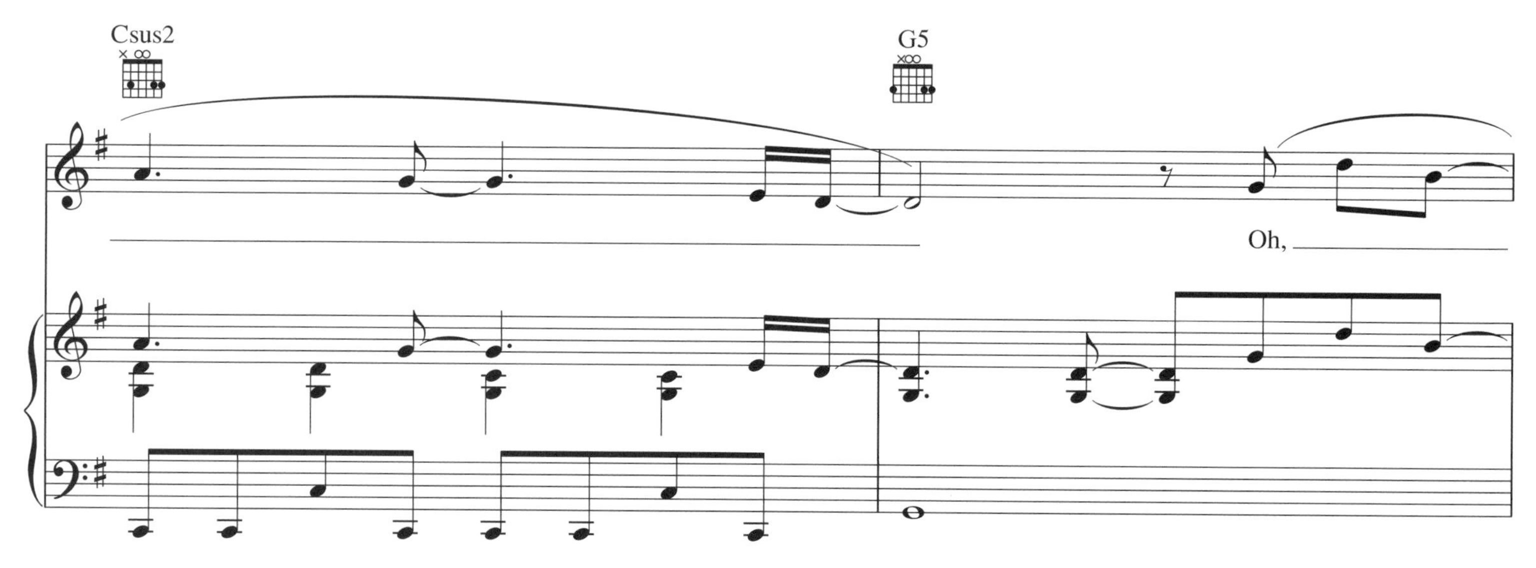
Csus2
G5
Oh,

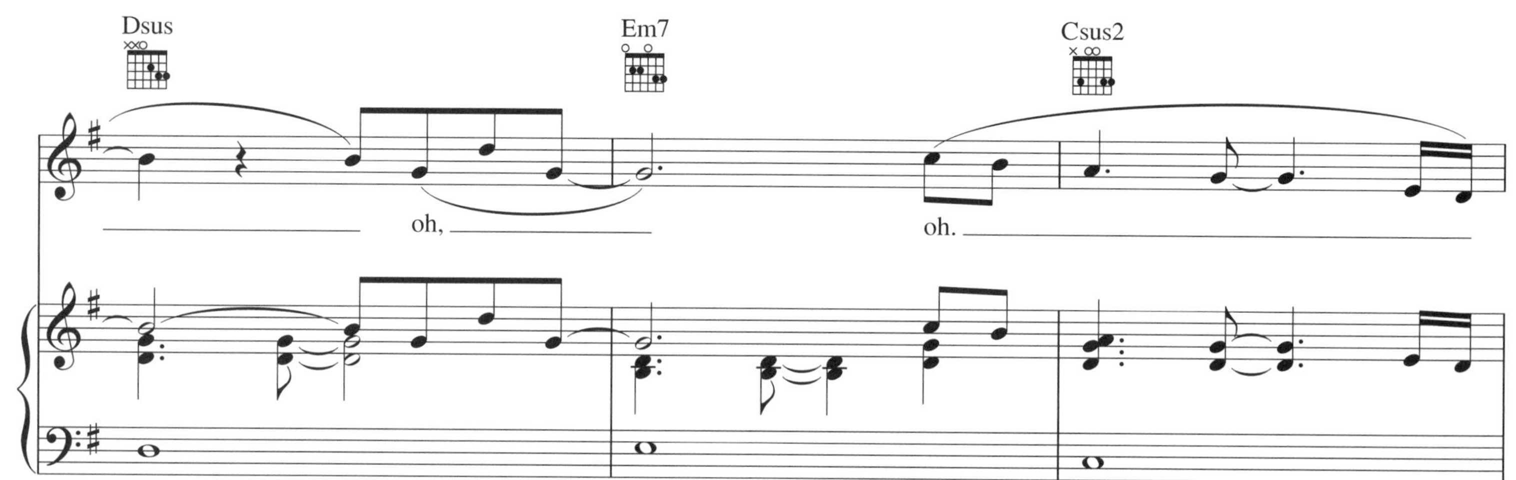
Dsus
Em7
Csus2
oh,
oh.

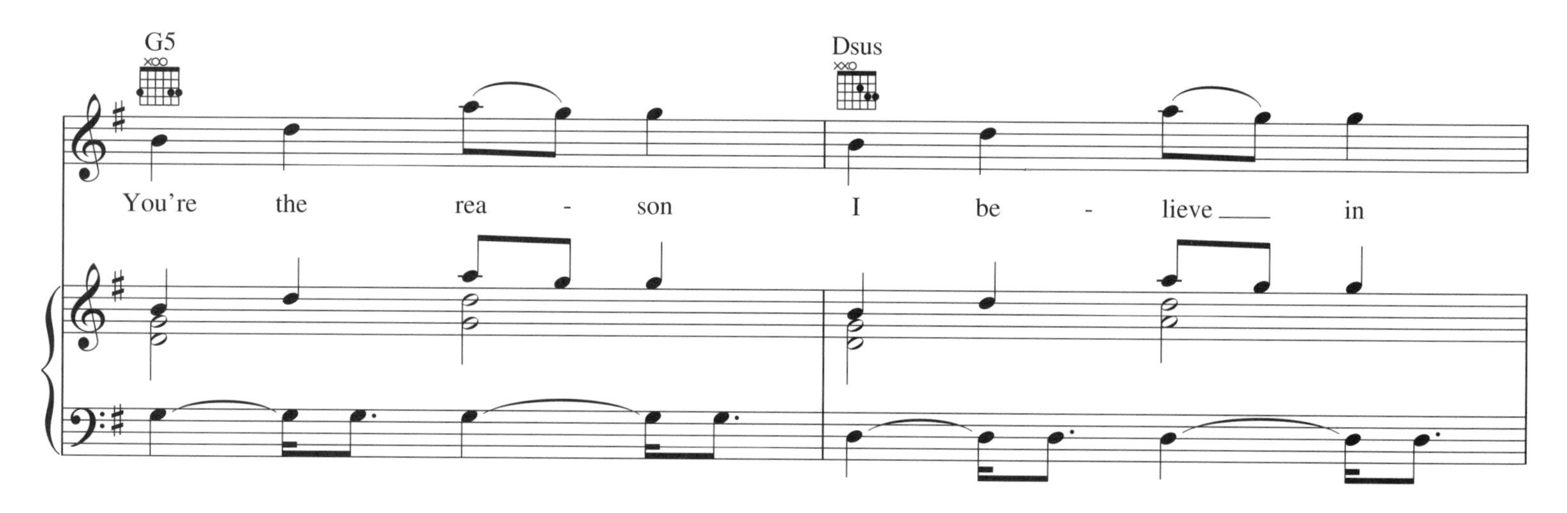
G5
Dsus
You're the rea - son I be - lieve in

Em
C(add9)
some - thing I don't know.

HAZEL

Words and Music by
PHILLIP PHILLIPS

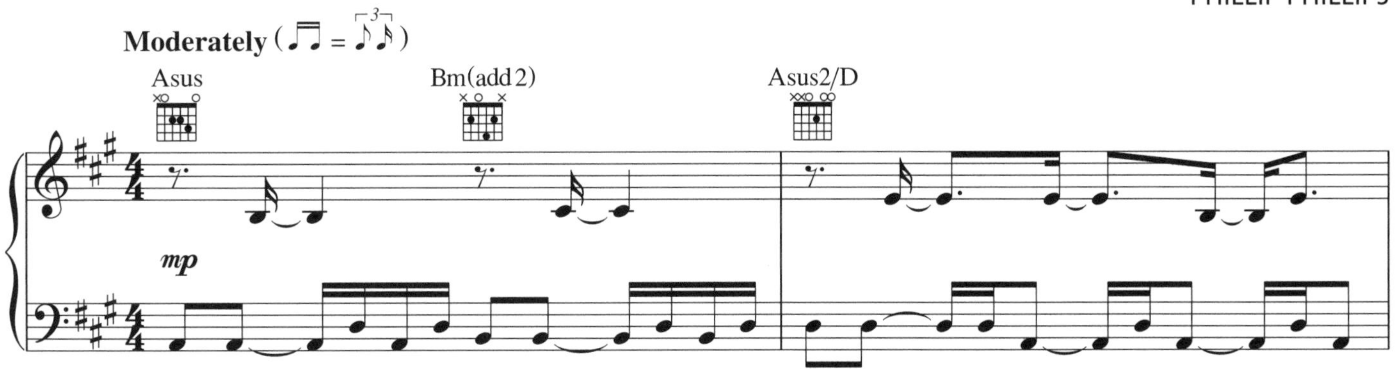

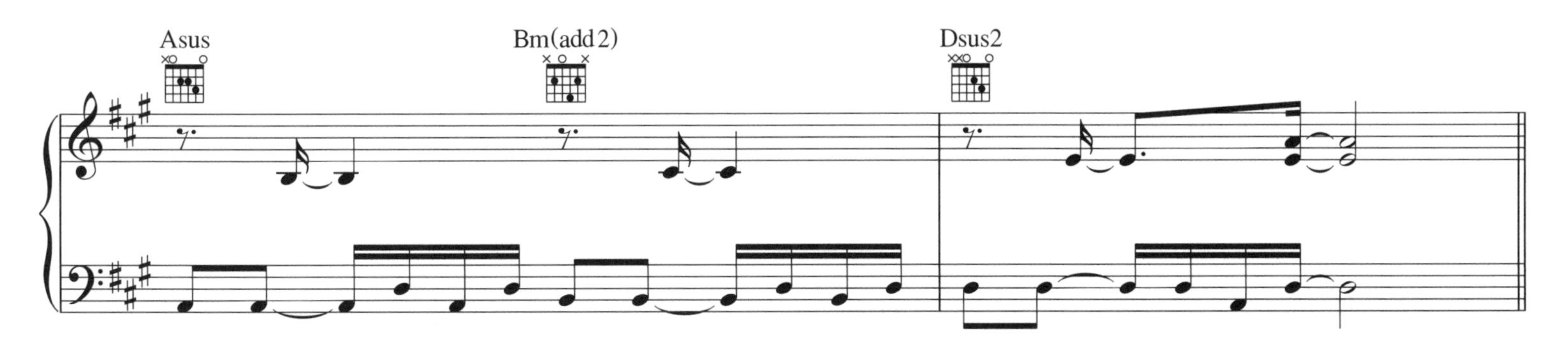

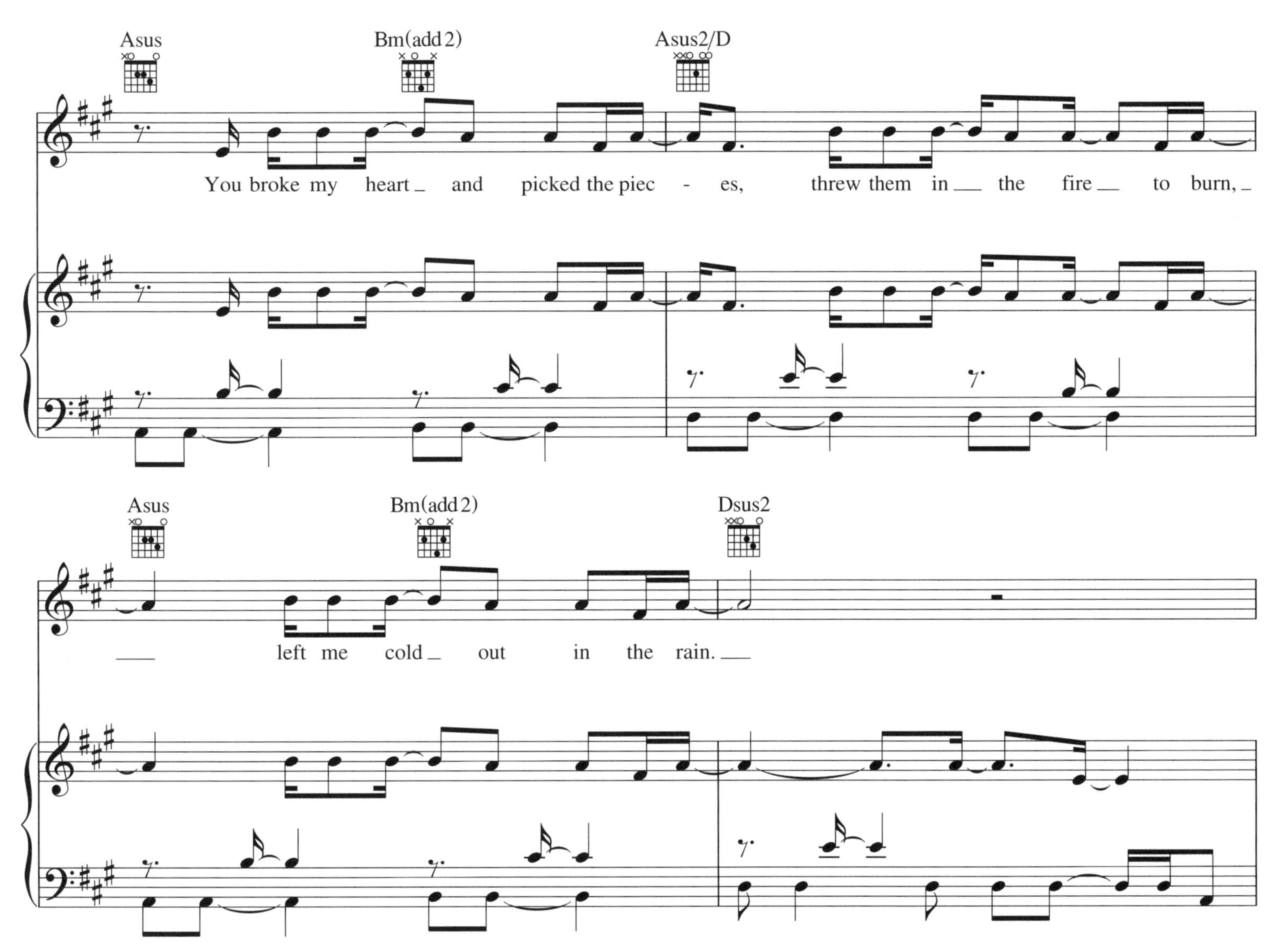

Asus
Bm(add2)
Asus2/D
But now I'm mov - ing on without you, ba - by, with-out you by my side;
Asus
Bm(add2)
Dsus2
I'm fi - nal - ly feel - ing free.
A/C♯
Bm
D5
E5/D
D5
5fr
2fr
5fr
But I know that the sun will shine for me,
A/C♯
Bm
D5
Dsus2
5fr
e - ven when the skies are grey.

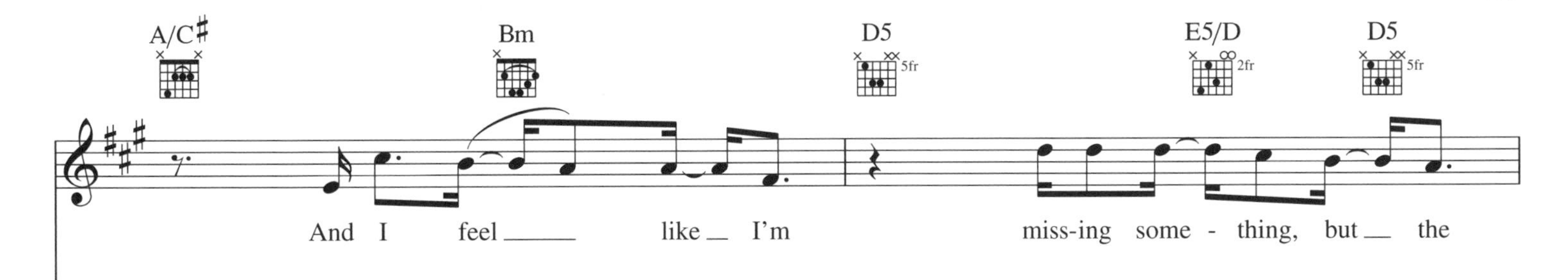
A/C♯
Bm
D5
5fr
E5/D
2fr
D5
5fr
And I feel ___ like _ I'm miss-ing some - thing, but _ the

A/C♯
Bm
D5
5fr
bridg - es build _ their _ own way. ___

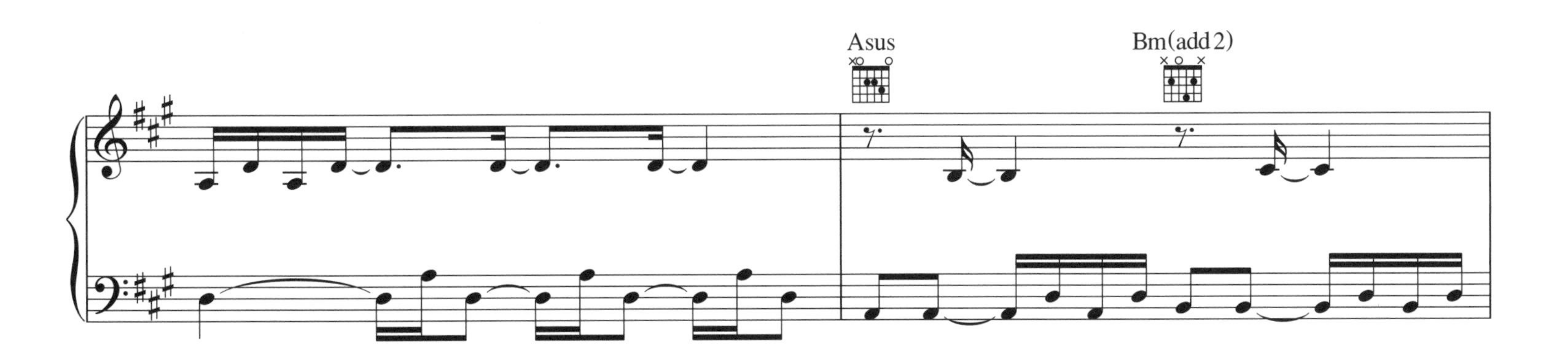
Asus
Bm(add2)

Asus2/D
Asus
Bm(add2)

Dsus2
Asus
Bm(add2)
I know you've moved on with-out me, girl,
Asus2/D
Asus
Bm(add2)
but I still think how the time, it moves so
Dsus2
Asus
Bm(add2)
fast.
I still think of how the world,
Asus2/D
Asus
Bm(add2)
it goes a-round and 'round and 'round;
but it all stopped when you said,

Dsus2
"Not for now."
A/C♯
Bm
D5
E5/D
D5
But I know that the sun will shine for me
A/C♯
Bm
D5
Dsus2
e-ven when the skies are grey.
A/C♯
Bm
D5
E5/D
D5
And I feel like I'm miss-ing some-thing, but the

A/C♯
Bm
D5
5fr
bridg - es build their own way.
E5/D
2fr
Like the o - cean wash - es the sand to the shore,
you're like the sun that slips a - way.
Lips that taste of an an - gel and eyes that bring me to my knees,

A/C#
Bm
D5
5fr
and a smile that could set me free.
A
E
Dsus2
Just fol - low me.
Just fol - low
A
E
Dsus2
A
E
me.
Just fol - low me, yeah,
Dsus2
A
E
Dsus2
oh.